MEDIUM RARE

JEANETTE WILSON

Zenith Publishing

Every effort has been taken to clear quotes used in this book with the person quoted. We apologise for any oversight in the regard that may have occurred inadvertently.

ISBN 1-877365-01-7

Zenith Publishing
PO Box 752
49-55 Rimu Street extn
New Plymouth
New Zealand
www.zenithpublishing.co.nz

First published in July 2004 by Zenith Publishing

Reprinted August & September 2004

Proudly printed in New Zealand by Publishing Press Ltd

Cover photograph by Sue Maxwell

To my grandparents
in Heaven with a
SMILE and a
HUG!

Contents

vi	About the Author
vii	Foreword
1	A Peculiar Feeling
25	Waking Up
43	We Are Not Alone
55	A Purpose
67	Looking for Answers
80	A Choice to Make
98	In Search of a Teacher
117	A New Career
144	Inner Peace
158	Money
172	Choosing a Partner
186	India
206	Is There Such a Thing as Fate?
220	A Family
235	A New Home
253	Accepting Responsibility
274	End Notes
275	Preview of Jeanette's Next Book

About the Author

Jeanette Wilson lives in Taranaki with her partner Andrew and their two children Sarah and Liam. Jeanette regularly tours New Zealand with her sell-out shows 'Jeanette Wilson – Live'. Jeanette's amazing gift enables her to bring messages from your loved ones that can touch your very soul, bring tears, hope, laughter and often the inspiration for you to see the world and your experiences with new eyes.

Her messages can bring a new acceptance and the courage to heal and to love ever more deeply despite all you have experienced.

Jeanette is passionate and clear about her role in the world; she is here as a teacher and a healer. Much of the profit from her shows goes to a trust (IRD approved) that amongst other things is actively involved in providing alternative education that encourages children to be all that they can be.

Jeanette is an active supporter of groups who oppose releasing GE into our environment and our food chain until it is fully tested. Jeanette is a firm believer in informed decision making. She encourages you to seek as much information as you can about any issue that concerns you so that you can make good, informed choices for yourselves and your children.

When she is not touring, Jeanette spends her time enjoying her family.

Foreword

I first started writing this book in response to the many requests I had received asking me to explain how I went from being a successful bank manager who was completely sceptical of mediums and clairvoyants to working as an international medium in front of large audiences around the world.

How did I start? How did I get my confidence? How did I know it wasn't just my imagination? Why did I give up a rewarding and successful career to do something that many people would regard as frivolous nonsense?

I intended to self publish this, my first book, and make it available at my shows to answer some of the questions that there was never time to answer during the two hour demonstrations of mediumship. Within hours of the first draft being ready a local publisher contacted me to see if I would like to be published. They studied my first draft and concluded quite rightly that it was four books in one. I had attempted to tell the story of how I became a medium, explain how to tap into your intuition, how to speak to loved ones in spirit world and how to advance spiritually all at once. They tactfully pointed out that the first book logically would be about how I made the transformation from sceptical bank manager to international medium and asked me to write about just that.

I wasn't sure if I was ready to tell that story. A lot of the things that have happened to me sound 'odd' even now. Some things I hadn't told anyone, not even my partner. How should I start to explain phenomena I had never even heard of before? How could I explain the things that happened in ways people could cope with and somehow comprehend? And how would I feel about complete strangers reading and judging my heartfelt truth? To my surprise the story came out easily, helped by diaries I have kept over the past ten years. In no time the entire new book, this book, was written.

There are parts where I could have taken an entire chapter to explain my thoughts and feelings or my experiences. This was not possible. What I have tried to achieve is an overview of my journey to this point and plan to expand in more depth in some areas in subsequent books.

At mediumship shows the people attending tend to fall into three categories. People who believe in life after death, perhaps because of their own experiences, people who are open-minded about the possibility of life after death and people who are sceptical of there being life after death. It seems reasonable to assume that readers of this book may also fall into any one of these three categories. Ten years ago I was very firmly in the sceptical category. Today as a direct result of my personal experiences I am in the believing category and I spend my life demonstrating to the best of my ability that there is no death. Why? Because I know that there is no death, and I also know that I am able to prove this on a consistent basis. Do I do it then because I can? No. I do it because I choose to.

When we know that there is no death, that we are eternal, our whole life transforms as mine did. I am infinitely more peaceful and happier than I was before. Ask yourself; if you had discovered something that would make people more peaceful and happier would you want to share it? Would your wanting to share it override your fear of ridicule or embarrassment? What if you had experienced some really weird phenomena that people may not believe, may even laugh at? Would you still put what you knew into the public domain?

I guess my love for humanity is stronger than my fear of personal discomfort these days. Perhaps the past ten years have a lot to answer for.

Enjoy!

A Peculiar Feeling

As I rushed into the station I looked at my watch. Only four minutes until my train left. I'd cut it fine tonight. As I headed towards the platform I was suddenly overcome by a burning desire to buy a pen and paper. I scanned the station. Yes there was a bookseller, but a long queue of dark-suited commuters waited to buy their evening papers. I checked my watch again. I knew that if I missed the train there would be at least an hour's wait for the next one. I was hungry and tired and desperate to get home, but something still drove me to join the queue.

It had been a long day. Travelling by train and tube, I'd had to leave early to get to my course at the training venue at Regent's College in the heart of London. I did not enjoy travelling into London, racing other commuters for a seat on the train by dirty windows you could barely see out of and if that failed standing for the whole journey. Commuters, their faces in newspapers or, like me, not knowing quite where to look. It was an awkward situation and made me feel uncomfortable. The tube was even worse with people pressed up against me. At five feet four inches, I was too short to hold the ceiling handles and occasionally the only thing that kept me vertical was the pressure of other commuters' bodies around me.

This morning's whole unpleasant journey had taken almost two hours. Thankfully, I only travelled into London when I had to for work or when there was something special I really wanted to do.

This time, it was for both reasons. I had been keen to do a Neuro Linguistic Programming course after I had witnessed a trainer using it. I could see the benefits both personally and professionally. I had asked the bank to send me on the course and finally they had agreed. So here I was returning from my first day at Regent's College.

That first day on the course had brought with it mixed feelings. I was excited about finally getting to attend the course of my dreams and anxious about meeting the other sixty-three participants and what the course would really involve. What if I had to talk in front of such a large group? What if they all knew more than me or had more experience than me? My thoughts had not been the most helpful and calming that morning.

The trainer had helped us all feel at ease right from the start and we had met the full training team, which included about a dozen training assistants. I liked the trainer's style and had learnt a lot on the first day. We had worked for the main part in small groups, which had eased my fears about talking in front of the large group. Now the first day was over, I was feeling more settled about the course and was keen to get home for my evening meal.

But the long train journey home loomed ahead. It would be after 7:30 pm before I got home to start preparing a meal. My stomach rumbled; I wished I had eaten more at lunchtime. I definitely didn't want to miss this train.

Yet, the urge remained. Why must I buy a notebook and pen? I couldn't understand it. I had been resisting it because I doubted whether I would have time to buy them and still make my train! An internal battle raged for a few moments; then I couldn't resist it anymore. I strode to the bookseller's kiosk and joined the queue, pen and notebook in hand; a notebook I still have to this day.

With relief I reached my train, just as it set off. I had very nearly missed it. I was grateful that the seat next to me was free for a change. It meant there would be no distractions and I would have time to reflect on the day.

Once the train had accelerated to a steady pace I took my notebook out of the paper bag and started to write. I had an extremely strong inner feeling that I had to record events as they happened and that something was about to happen to me that was important and would change my life.

I put a name at the top of each of the pages in the notebook; the name of the trainer and the names of people I'd got to know that first day and I began writing about them. I didn't know why I was suddenly driven to record my experiences. I'd not kept a diary before. But this is how the journey began for me, ten years ago, when I was thirty-one.

From my role as a bank manager at Lloyds Bank – the most traditional of the United Kingdom's High Street banks – I was about to be hurtled into a world I knew nothing about. I was to go through such monumental changes in my thinking that my way of seeing the world was going to change forever. This is the story of how that all happened.

I had joined Lloyds Bank at sixteen rather than stay on at school to do 'A' levels. I was a bright student and everyone at school was surprised when I didn't stay on to study further. Why didn't I? Mainly, I was frightened of the prospect of going to university and being away from home. In my mind also was the knowledge that in 'A' level biology I would need to dissect a mouse. We had kept mice as pets and I liked them. Why, I thought, should animals be killed, one for each class member, when we could see what their insides looked like from textbooks? I would perhaps have been a doctor, had it been possible to train without dissecting animals along the way. I wasn't squeamish about it – it just seemed fundamentally wrong to kill another living thing without good reason.

In England, if you didn't go to university and wanted a career rather than a job your choices boiled down to working for a utility company such as the power, gas, phone or water company, working for the government or working for a bank. Lloyds Bank, Park Row, Leeds was where I went for my first interview.

In earlier years I used to pass the branch on my way to the international swimming pool. The bank was situated just off City Square in the centre of Leeds. Park Row housed the city's main banks and insurance companies. It was where you found the most impressive corporate buildings in Leeds.

Lloyds Bank, Park Row was a breathtaking eight floors of expensive-looking brown marble. An eye-catching, cast iron sculpture of a black horse stood proudly at the front, dominating Park Row. It was undoubtedly the most prestigious building I had ever seen. As a teenager, I had naively thought that it would be so cool to work somewhere like that.

It was strange, on the day of that first interview, to be walking in the door of a building I had walked past so many times before. A uniformed man on the front desk directed me to Personnel. I took the lift up to the seventh floor. Two men joined me as the lift stopped on the third floor. As they stood with me in that confined space they joked about the cashiers on the ground floor and how they were all female, attractive and well-endowed. The younger of the two joked it was part of the selection criteria that they had at least thirty-six inch busts. I blushed and looked at the floor. I hadn't heard people talk like this before and they clearly weren't bothered about talking this way in front of me; a young girl.

I was glad when the lift stopped at the seventh floor and I could get out. I introduced myself at reception and went through into the waiting area. I sat there nervously for what seemed like an eternity. I felt odd in my suit. It reminded me a bit of my school blazer. Mum had made me get a suit for the interview reasoning that I would need it anyway when I started work. It wasn't my choice but I supposed it looked okay. I couldn't wait to earn my own money so I could buy the clothes I wanted. My smile tensed again as I remembered where I was; at my first ever job interview. I would be glad when it was over I thought as I wondered why they hadn't taught me anything like interview practice at school.

My thoughts were interrupted by a friendly-looking man emerging from the room in front of me. He confirmed my name and then introduced himself as the assistant personnel manager for the region. He would be conducting the interview. He had an informal manner and I soon started to feel at ease. He couldn't understand why I wasn't going on to 'A' levels and then university. I said I was keen to study while working for the bank. He seemed happy enough with the response and said that I would probably want to go on their management programme. This would mean spending a year or two in each job and doing exams as I went, he explained. It sounded good to me as I had a tendency to get bored easily. He offered me the job on the spot and said I could start the following week. I agreed and was taken through to meet another manager. My face must have been a picture. It was the younger man from the lift. I guess I must have met the selection criteria!

Working in a bank was not as I had expected, however. I started in what was very aptly called the 'machine room'. There a group of girls sorted cheques into alphabetical order and worked on computers. I had naively assumed I would be working as a cashier, but that, I discovered later, would be years away.

I spent the first twelve months just sorting cheques into alphabetical order before I worked my way up to sitting at one of the computers. Some girls had sorted cheques for years. I vowed that I would not allow that to happen to me. One day I would be a bank manager. In my logical brain I reasoned that if I had to work, and it seemed that everyone did, I'd rather be paid managers' wages than clerks' wages.

Fortunately the social life in the bank more than made up for the boredom of the work I was doing. Bankers are often not as boring as they at first appear. I was earning reasonably good money for someone my age and still living at home. I was enjoying having my own money for the first time, so I stayed on.

As time went by I started to notice downsides, particularly that there seemed to me to be little room for flexibility or individuality. For example, at one time I had my hair permed. I admit my hair has never permed well, but I was shocked to be called into the manager's office and told in no uncertain terms that it was not suitable for a bank employee! Such conservatism; I wasn't even in contact with the public at that time. I was only working in the machine room. During the time I worked in the machine room, the only young man recruited into the department was moved out within weeks to more senior duties while another very capable girl with an ethnic background stayed sorting cheques in the machine room long after I had come and gone from that department.

At my appointment interview I had been promised time off to do further study and banking exams but for what seemed ages, it didn't materialise. The machine room was busy and I was needed, so I initially had to study in my own time. It was only after one of the managers called me in to see him that I felt that the bank realised I had some potential. The manager asked if I was going to go to the Yorkshire and Humberside regional dinner. I was. He told me to wear my 'best bib and tucker'. I presumed he meant my best clothes. When I asked why, he claimed he couldn't tell me but then proceeded to confide that I had got the best exam results for the whole of the Yorkshire and Humberside region. Consequently I would be receiving an award at the dinner. He urged that I must keep it quiet and act surprised when the announcement was made. Sure enough, at the dinner, I received the award but even that didn't get me promoted onto the management programme or to cashier that I felt had been promised at my first interview.

After about six months I was finally admitted to the management programme and things slowly started to change though I felt I had to continually prove myself at every turn. To get into management, I had to go through the securities department and learn how to lend. The securities department of a branch is not as you might imagine. It's not like Securicor or Armour

Guard. It is the section that lends money and does all the paperwork to secure lending such as mortgages and guarantees. The whole department at the Leeds branch was male and they seemed to me a bit of a traditional group. They earned more than anyone except the managers and someone had once told me that they had never known a woman to work in the securities department. I could see that this was going to be a challenge.

Eventually, however, my hard work paid off. After three years of study and the completion of my banking exams I made it into the securities department. Imagine my irritation when I finally got there and found that almost all of the men there were still working on their exams. Only two had actually completed them. I felt cheated, but I said nothing, kept my head down and got on with the work.

At least I was in securities at last and there was a lot to learn, from stocks and shares through to money market deposits. A few months passed and I was doing very well in the securities department. My line manager was pleased with me. I knew that very soon I would be learning how to lend money, or so I thought. Rather than move me onto lending which they had to do quite soon to meet my management programme, the management announced that they wanted me to transfer to another branch. After only nine months in the securities department this was quite disappointing. But tradition was restored; the securities department was all male again.

My boss, one of three at the new branch, seemed okay to begin with, but I soon noticed tension between him and the senior manager. It was uncomfortable to work in such a strained atmosphere and once again I was the only female in an all male department. I wasn't really enjoying it, so after eighteen months I was delighted when the senior manager called me in to say that I was on the short list for a job making training videos at Hindhead – the bank's training centre in Surrey. He asked if I would be interested if I was offered the job. I let him know that I was more than keen.

I talked it over with my partner. We had been living together for a couple of years and we had a committed relationship. He originally came from the south of England and was keen to move back there. He decided to start looking for jobs in case my promotion came about. Not long after, he was offered a job before me and so I put in for a transfer to the south of England in the interim. Oxford branch was looking for a lending assistant and I arranged to transfer there.

How refreshing it was to find a securities team of men and women and to find that they worked well together. The managers seemed good too. After I had been at Oxford for a couple of months I decided I had better ask about the training video job at Hindhead. My line manager knew nothing about it and nor did the senior manager. As far as they were concerned, I was with the branch on a permanent basis. It was a few years later that I found out that the lady who had got the job was called Janet Wilson as opposed to Jeanette Wilson. The job had never been mine, but it led to me being at Oxford and I was much happier even though I missed my family in Yorkshire.

I began to learn about making advances and it was not as easy as I thought it would be. It wasn't just a logical mathematical exercise. Emotions were involved; your's and the customer's. They didn't teach you this on the training courses. I found it really hard to say 'no', but reasoned with myself that I had to or I would get into trouble. As a woman it was very easy to overcompensate for this – to change from a 'soft lender' to become 'hard' – too ready to say 'no' before you had really listened to the customers.

At that time in the bank, records were kept on loans made by each manager that had 'gone bad' or not been repaid. These records were called bad debt cards. If you had a clean bad debt card you got promoted more easily. If you lent any money that went 'bad', it would go on your record card. It took the bank a few years to work out that some managers were keeping their bad debt cards clear by not lending money. This was a simple enough strategy but it meant that over time the managers who never lent any money got themselves into senior positions. Once there, they were authorised to lend huge sums of money but they really didn't know how to lend money. It was a recipe for disaster.

The good lenders lower down in the organisation who had not been promoted because they had accrued some bad debts, had to ask these senior managers to approve their lending. The senior managers would turn them down because that was how they kept their bad debt cards clean. The bank's lending portfolio was diminishing.

Targets were set and then even higher ones again. Still the bank's lending portfolio diminished. Eventually someone realised what was happening and came up with the solution of getting rid of the bad debt records, although no one ever quite believed that the debt cards had really been destroyed.

Lending was quite a stressful activity, whichever way you looked at it. I remember a male colleague, a really nice guy, had a baby left in the interview room by a customer when he turned down a request for borrowing. "You feed her because I can't!" the customer said as he walked out.

My own most difficult time came when I had to take a wages cheque off a customer and press a personal attack button to get colleagues to come in before he was able to physically attack me. He was evicted from the premises, but I found him waiting for me after work and then again in my local pub, which was miles away from the bank and nowhere near where he lived. I often wondered if it was worth it.

I did well at Oxford, however, and soon my manager was recommending me for promotion. He was very impressed with my work but felt I could do with more confidence. For that reason he had recommended me for a job at the regional training centre in Aylesbury. I cringed. I didn't like the idea of standing up in front of people. He explained that it would be a promotion and showed me my new salary as an assistant manager. I took the job and I met my best manager ever; a woman!

Sandra was the Personnel Manager. She inspired me like no other manager had done before. She took an interest in me and helped me work through my fears. She was a friend and a boss and knew how to differentiate the two. She taught me not to think about how I was feeling when I was nervous but instead to think about the people attending the workshop who were nervous too. They didn't know what to expect. I did! I had the trainer notes. If I worked on putting the attendees at ease I would put myself at ease too. It worked and I came first to enjoy training and then to love it. The feedback from participants was wonderful. They loved coming to my workshops. I got chocolates, flowers, bottles of wine and even a yellow fluffy chick that said, "You're a Quacker." to thank me for the workshops. My confidence grew and grew.

Soon, however, it would be time for me to go back into a branch.

In the bank at that time you had two assistant manager appointments before becoming a manager. One might be in something different like training, money market or foreign exchange, but one had to be in a branch in readiness for being a manager. I hadn't given my next position much thought as I was thoroughly enjoying what I was doing.

I didn't have to look for my next job though. It found me. The senior manager at Oxford branch wanted me back as Assistant Manager – Sales, a new role that he had created and the first of its type in the bank. The only thing was, he was now Area Director and I would be working for the new manager at Oxford branch, who I had never met before. I heard on the grapevine that he did not suffer fools well but had an excellent reputation as a manager. I was appalled to find that he would not be given the opportunity to interview me prior to my appointment or even to meet me. I would be imposed on him and I was expected to perform to an annual sales target of half a million pounds starting from ground zero. My alarm bells were ringing. If I was senior manager of a branch I would want to be consulted about the recruitment of a member of my management team. How did the manager feel about the situation? What if I didn't get on with him? How would I meet the astronomical sales target without the support of the senior manager of the branch?

Although I had some reservations I accepted the job, as I had always loved a challenge. I had friends at the Oxford branch and much preferred to go back there than into a new branch with people I didn't know.

My first contact with John, Senior Manager, seemed to go well but I couldn't be sure. Sometimes people don't express their true feelings if someone is controlling them from higher up. However confirmation came an hour later when he phoned me.

"Miss Wilson, do you see the tanker on Carfax?" I could see a double tanker trying to negotiate Carfax Corner just outside the window. "A fiver says he won't make it!" he said. I laughed and I knew I was going to get on with John just fine.

There were gradual changes in the bank's working practices. Available job positions were now openly advertised and anyone could apply as opposed to what happened previously, when you were told where you were going next, or not as the case might be.

My life at Oxford was challenging and rewarding. It was a unique role and gave me many opportunities to motivate staff and teach new skills. I felt I had finally found my niche. However, I knew that eventually my time at Oxford would come to an end as my next job would be as a manager; that elusive dream I had set myself when I was sorting cheques into alphabetical order. I wasn't about to miss the opportunity when it came.

An assistant manager friend asked if I would be applying for the job at Hindhead. They were looking for a manager in charge of sales training. With my experience in sales and in training it sounded ideal. Try as I might I couldn't find the job advert. My management colleagues had decided to keep it from me for fear that if I saw it they may lose me. If the branch reached its sales target we all got bonuses. If I left they had a good chance of missing their targets and they would get nothing. When I went in search of the job advert they had to come clean and hand it over.

The job description might as well have had my name on it. I knew it was my job. I wanted to cry and laugh and scream at the same time. The managers also knew they would be losing me very soon. The Area Director was not pleased. Losing me would also affect his targets.

I travelled down from Leeds to Hindhead in Surrey for the interview; a car journey of about four hours. The training centre was set in beautiful grounds and had an excellent reputation. I had stayed there before as part of my management training. I was given a tour and invited to meet some of the existing trainers before being interviewed. The interview with two managers went well and I got the job. I found myself in my first managerial position at twenty-nine; a feat for anyone in the bank at that time but especially so for a woman. My colleagues congratulated me, as I was the first and only woman they knew of to reach a manager's position through the bank's management programme. Although I worried how they would react, I needn't have. They each let me know in their own way just how proud they were that I had apparently beaten the system; a woman and a non-university-graduate in management.

I remember phoning my father to let him know that my application had been successful. I was at last a bank manager. I could hear the emotion in his voice. He was so proud of me. I could hear the emotion in my own; it was not full of the joy I had expected. I felt empty and hollow. I suddenly realised for the first time, that I didn't want to be a bank manager. I had thought it was what my father had always wanted for me. It is funny how sometimes we don't know the right decision until we make the wrong one and then we feel it in our gut. This was how it was for me. I had worked for thirteen years and studied for seven years of them, in subjects I found thoroughly boring, to get somewhere in the bank, only to find it wasn't where I wanted to be. I did not want to be a bank manager. Not one little bit. Having reached this realisation I also realised that now I was able to set my own goals.

The consolation was that my first managerial appointment was as a 'Training Manager' and I decided that if I was to continue working for the bank it would need to be on the training side of the business. Perhaps because I knew so many talented colleagues who weren't fulfilling their potential, I became genuinely interested in helping people achieve more. I spent the next couple of years working at the bank's staff training college at Hindhead then moved onto the Management Centre at Kingswood in Surrey. At last I was doing something I truly enjoyed. Nerve-racking though it was to have to stand up in front of groups of people I didn't know, it beat working in a branch. It was more in alignment with who I was, so I excelled in the role, which was reflected in my annual performance reviews.

My line manager understood my constant striving for self-development though he often had to remind me that not everyone was as passionate about self-development as I was.

One of my main roles was to inspire, motivate, persuade, coerce or nag older managers, forty years and upwards, to sell. The bank had set insurance sales targets for the first time and so they sent the managers and staff on training workshops to assist them to achieve these. For some staff, this was the first time they had been asked to actively sell. Often the issue wasn't that the managers didn't know what to do. It was a motivational problem; they just didn't want to do it. They didn't feel they had joined the bank to sell. If they had wanted to sell insurance, they would claim, they would have joined an insurance company. If I had been given a pound for each time I heard that, I would not have needed to work.

I was given one week to turn their attitude around. To assist me in this somewhat daunting task an external trainer from a training consultancy would join me. The workshop was already written; all I had to do was deliver it! But it was no wonder they were paying the salary they were. I had to earn every penny.

All I can say is thank heaven for that external trainer. Some of those managers could and would have eaten me alive! The external trainer took the brunt of the negativity and aggression on the first day and was able to empathise with them because he came from outside the organisation. I was used for target practice! It seemed every time I opened my mouth I got jumped on. Who was I to tell them anything? Had I managed a branch? How old was I exactly? If they weren't saying it I could still see it in their eyes.

I was starting to worry that I had taken on too much. Things came to a head when the usual external trainer wasn't available. I got the news that they would be sending me a female replacement; a lady called Beverley Navarro.

I knew then what it was to be stressed. I met Beverley briefly before the workshop and we started to talk through how we would work together. She seemed competent enough but did she know what she was letting herself in for? Images of Christians being thrown to lions flashed before my eyes.

The workshop began and as usual, straight away there was negativity, resistance and outright mockery. Though the groups were usually comprised of older men, this one contained a younger man and his attacks were particularly vicious. But Beverley just said a few words to him and I witnessed what looked like a ripple going through his body and his whole outlook and demeanour changed. He became positive, encouraging and supportive. She did the same kind of thing with others. The words she spoke would be different but the effect would be the same. One by one they all changed their outlook. It was almost magical to observe.

How did she do that? I wanted to know. I wanted to be able to do it myself.

Beverley explained that she had trained in NLP (Neuro Linguistic Programming). If I wanted to know more she suggested getting a book called 'Influencing with Integrity' by Genie Z Laborde. I ordered it as soon as I could and read it from cover to cover. It was fascinating.

I found out that 'Neuro' refers to the brain and the neurological pathways that are activated when we think. 'Linguistic' refers to the language we use when we think, and 'Programming' to how we have programmed ourselves either consciously or unconsciously. Simply put, when I say or think the word 'Christmas', for example, I trigger within myself a response of feelings, memories and related thoughts. Similarly if I talk to you about 'Christmas' I will trigger within you your programmed responses. By becoming more aware of our programming we can start to recognise which programming is useful and which we could choose to move beyond. NLP is basically a tool for helping us to better understand ourselves as well as others.

More than ever, I wanted to be able to do what I had seen Beverley do. I researched the different training companies offering NLP training and put a case forward to my line manager for me to attend a course. The training, I discovered, would last five weeks and cost over five thousand pounds. I used what little I knew of NLP to influence my line manager to send me on the course. It was an uphill struggle. Usually no more than one thousand pounds was allocated for external training and at most two weeks were allowed for it. My line manager politely turned down my request. He turned me down the next year too. Five thousand pounds and five weeks were just too much to ask.

After three rounds of pestering, however, some may call it nagging, my persistence finally paid off. I was at the end of my appointment to the Management Centre and about to take up my second managerial post as Training Manager for the North of England, based in Leeds when my line manager asked for a word with me.

Somehow he had managed to get me approval to attend the NLP training. I would be doing two courses over five weeks; all that I had asked for. My heart sang. The course was partly as a reward for all my hard work and the contribution I had made to the centre and partly to find out if NLP would benefit our training business. I would be expected to report to the bank when I returned, on the potential value of NLP to the organisation.

As a trainer I could see a great many applications for NLP in my work. As an individual I really wanted to be able to use it on myself. I had become interested in being all that I could be. I was highly self-motivated – 'driven' my mother would call it – and I always tried my best. At last I would have access to the tool I had been looking for.

Would NLP help me to manifest my full potential?

Waking Up

The timing of the Neuro Linguistic Programming course was quite awkward in that I would be taking up my new appointment in Leeds for only one week before disappearing for five weeks back to London for the course. My new manager was not impressed. His reactions were a mix of questions and comments; what was this NLP stuff anyway? The time I was to spend at the course had better be worthwhile. Why couldn't I have done the training when the Training Centre employed me? Was it really essential? How much was it costing again? I was glad it had already been paid for and booked; otherwise I suspect I might not have been able to go.

The course was at Regent's College, which is set in Regent's Park. To see such a beautiful and peaceful park in the heart of London took me by surprise. It was the perfect setting and it meant we were able to work outdoors for much of the time.

There were sixty-four participants on the course from a wide range of backgrounds, ranging from myself, a bank manager, through to accountants, self-employed business people and people working for charitable organisations such as Greenpeace. We truly were a mixed bunch, but we had one thing in common; we all wanted to reach our highest potential and were prepared to take time out to do just that. Most of those attending had paid for themselves, which was particularly impressive and greatly enhanced their commitment to the course.

In the ensuing days, I was pleased to find it was easy to make friends with other people on the course. We were all in the same boat; nervous, curious and not knowing quite what we had let ourselves in for. It was not the kind of course where you could just sit back. We were all actively involved from day one; actively finding out who everyone else was, actively exploring why we were like we were and how we could easily and effortlessly change ourselves if we wanted to, merely by altering our ways of thinking about things.

The training assistants were approachable, friendly and skilled at what they did; especially at giving feedback. They stretched us whilst still respecting our feelings and nervousness. It was good to remember how it felt to be on the receiving end of training. I had almost forgotten.

Three days into the workshop I learned something about myself I hadn't realised before. I realised that I never, ever asked anyone for help. I had seen it as a sign of weakness. I now understood that in some areas of life I might need to ask for help; it was a wise thing to do. I made a commitment to myself to ask for help when I needed it. Was this a trigger for what happened in the next few days? I do not know. Something was, because it wasn't very long after that, that I did need to ask for help – big time!

Another technique that was to become significant was one we were taught that is used to help you identify any 'part' of you that is preventing the fulfilment of the whole. By talking to the 'part' (internalising it) and understanding its motivation you can negotiate a way forward that will keep all parts of you happy and help you achieve your goals.

On the fourth day the trainer asked me if I would volunteer for an exercise. I hesitated, making sure he meant me. He wanted me to stand in front of over sixty people and do what exactly? Part of me froze. That part of me just did not want to stand up there. But the potential embarrassment of refusing his polite request seemed worse than the potential embarrassment of what might happen.

I went forward rather anxiously and stood in front of the group. So many eyes looked at me.

"Close your eyes," guided the trainer. I did as I was told. I was much happier with my eyes closed than seeing the other participants looking at me.

The trainer explained that he wanted to use me to demonstrate because my face was very expressive. The exercise we were about to explore was to practise getting into emotional states that were useful to us. (We can all get into un-useful emotional states at the drop of a hat.) This was a way of being able to take charge of our emotional states, consciously and effectively managing their impact upon us. Any new feeling would probably be better than how I was feeling standing in front of the group, so I was happy to assist.

"What emotional state would you like to experience?" asked the trainer.

'Joy' immediately sprang to mind and popped out of my mouth. Joy it was.

The trainer took me through a series of steps and each time the emotion intensified until very soon I was bursting with joy. I completely forgot I was standing in front of a group. All I could feel was joy. It was wonderful!

"Would you like to intensify the feeling?" asked the trainer.

"No, I think I would burst," I replied and a ripple of laughter went through the room.

"What would happen if you did?" teased the trainer. I didn't respond. I was in a completely blissful state; no words could explain how I felt. I couldn't imagine intensifying the feeling any more.

I couldn't stop smiling and felt like I was glowing. Many of the group came over to me and said how amazing the transformation within me was. I was bursting with joy and practically floated out of class that day. I felt totally confident.

The next morning I could still feel the sense of joy but it was not as strong – try as I might I couldn't recapture the amazing feeling of the day before. The first activity of the morning was an exercise related to a further exploration of the 'part' of ourselves that holds us back. The trainer asked for volunteers to participate in a demonstration. As volunteers were being chosen, I became aware that I could feel a hard lump in the middle of my chest. It was dense and walnut-shaped. As I moved my awareness into it, I suddenly realised that when I had experienced 'joy' the day before there had been a limitation on my experience. I had feared 'bursting'. It was as though my joy had been contained by a giant membrane extending a couple of metres from my body. The membrane that had been light and elastic then, was now shrivelled up and had formed a hard lump in my chest. I didn't understand why that should be and tried desperately to understand.

The lump was tired and confused. It wanted me to draw attention to it. It wanted me to volunteer. When I didn't, it started to get annoyed with me. These feelings were coming from inside me rather than as rational thoughts and I was reluctant to volunteer because I was afraid of what would happen. It was very strange. As the demonstration proceeded the 'part's' emotion suddenly changed to disappointment and then to total despair.

As soon as the break came, I went to the toilet and started to cry. I was embarrassed about crying in public. After a while, I tidied myself up and joined the coffee queue, only to find myself crying uncontrollably again. I had never cried so openly in my life before. I just couldn't stop the tears.

The trainer came over and I told him what I was feeling. I explained the emotions the 'part' was feeling; how it was despairing that I had not volunteered. I told him I had an increasingly definite sense that it was a 'he' and for some reason unknown to me at the time, I felt 'he' was my grandad. The very idea that this 'part' was actually my grandad was something new and quite unsettling to me but I rationalised it in the context of the course, and thought it was part of the NLP techniques; that this was just an expected outcome of the exercise. When the session restarted the trainer asked me to sit closer to the front so he could keep an eye on me.

As I stood watching the final part of the exercise, but also wrestling with this strange set of feelings, the girl next to me, Jennifer, touched me on my arm and asked if I was okay. That gesture of concern was enough to start me crying again and so the two of us went outside. I explained to Jennifer what I was experiencing.

"How wonderful!" she exclaimed with real enthusiasm. At this response 'Grandad' seemed to grow a bit and glowed. It seemed to be a sign he wanted me to work with Jennifer. I now know that there is amazing synchronicity of events where things fall into place, the right person is there at the right time, and this was just one of those occasions. Jennifer was that 'right' person.

We found a quiet spot on the grass under the shade of a tree. I decided that I needed to lie down and Jennifer sat beside me. I began thinking about my grandad who had died when I was six. I hadn't been close to my grandad. He was a tall man who always commanded the respect of the family. He wasn't one for getting close to the grandchildren. I had only two clear memories of Grandad. The first was how he put salt on his porridge. As a child, that had terrified me. I had never known anybody to put salt on their porridge! The second was of him lying in what I now realise was his deathbed, looking gaunt and frail, with bony fingers.

If any person from my past were likely to be with me, I would have expected it to be my grandma. I was the apple of her eye. For her, I could do no wrong. We had a very special relationship and she passed away when I was thirteen. So I was wondering why Grandad was somehow with me, and why Grandma was not there too. But I was increasingly without doubt; 'Grandad' was here, talking to me, in my body and crying.

I can understand how people hearing this story will wonder how I could make a leap from conservative bank manager to accepting this 'spirit' form of my grandad without tipping my life into turmoil. But the vividness of this image of Grandad was so real I felt completely accepting of it. Weird as it may seem, I could see Grandad internally as a hologram of white light with his head perfectly formed and recognisable. I wasn't frightened at all.

The trainer came out to check on us. Jennifer explained the new developments. The trainer interpreted what Jennifer told him from an NLP point of view and suggested we talk to 'Grandad' as though he were a six-year-old child. In NLP it is thought that everyone has an 'inner child' with wants, needs and fears and you are encouraged to get in touch with them. Because I was attaching a person to the 'part', the trainer thought I must have been talking to my 'inner child'. I accepted then that this must be a normal part of the NLP training process. So Jennifer gently encouraged me to start talking to Grandad, to find out what he wanted.

It was a tricky start. Jennifer had to learn to talk to the child rather than to me directly. We had been learning as we unravelled ourselves on the course, that every part of ourselves should be presumed to have a positive intent. So she asked my Grandad-child what the positive intent was behind his behaviour.

"For Jeanette to be happy," came the reply from within me.

"How do you do this?" asked Jennifer.

"By protecting her from any bad feelings like embarrassment or ridicule," Grandad replied through me.

"Is there any other way you could do this?" Jennifer asked.

"Love."

"Any others?" asked Jennifer.

"A hug."

"Would you like to give Jeanette a hug now?" Jennifer asked.

My head nodded, and we hugged, my Grandad's spirit and mine embraced inside my body.

"Enjoy that hug," Jennifer encouraged, and after a few moments, "How did that feel?"

"Good, happy," came the reply and then suddenly alarm showed on Grandad's face. He shot away from me; there was a blinding flash of light.

Despair, horror and remorse all in one overwhelmed Grandad and then me. He realised he had made a dreadful mistake. Grandad explained that he'd been in my space since he had died. Instead of making the usual transition through to spirit world, he had stayed in my space because he had wanted to protect me. But he'd now come to realise that in doing so he had affected a number of choices I'd made in my life, perhaps even kept me from opportunities I would have loved and enjoyed. He had kept me from volunteering the day before and I remembered that I had felt a 'part' of me resisting. He didn't think I would like it in front of such a large group. But I had; I had experienced joy!

Now he was terribly, terribly sorry. He showed so much pain and remorse, and indicated that he should not have interfered with my life path in the way that he did.

Jennifer said, "Let your feelings go. Cry!"

A violent reaction coursed through me. Grandad was shaking his head, kicking his feet and shouting.

"No cry. No cry." said Grandad.

Jennifer soothed him and eventually he cried.

"Is there anyone there to help him?" Jennifer asked softly. Jennifer was a naturally sensitive person and this question, looking back, was quite inspired.

I suddenly became aware of another presence within me, again, inside my body, but this time it was

Grandma. I was so pleased to see her. Grandma had come for Grandad. In physical life, nothing had ever been the same for Grandma once Grandad died. They'd had a very good marriage, totally committed to one another. Nobody could have ever taken the place of Grandad. When Grandad died, there was always a part of Grandma that wanted to be with him and everybody in the family knew this, but she held on here for several years before she did eventually pass away.

At that time I didn't have the understanding to appreciate how we transition from here to the spirit world and that sometimes spirit can remain here. I now realise Grandma must have expected to find Grandad on the other side. Imagine her utter disbelief when on passing through into the spirit side of life, she found that Grandad wasn't there because he hadn't made the appropriate transition. He was still in my space, so she had been kept from Grandad for a further 18 years! Staying with me, Grandad would have retained a lower vibrational level than spirits in the normal spirit world. As I became more attuned and Grandad began to release himself from me, his vibrational level would have risen to a point where he became distinguishable to my grandma and she could connect with him.

You can imagine their delight at being reunited. My Grandma put her arms around Grandad while he sobbed.

I felt very close to both of them and privileged to be sharing this moment with them.

Eventually Grandad looked up. He wanted me to give my father a message. Jennifer, who was thinking much more clearly than I was at this time, asked him how he could help me ensure my father knew the message came from him. It was a really good question. Grandad looked at me and beckoned me to a door at the far right of a room. He opened it and I saw the Bolehills, in Sheffield, near where we used to live. He laughed heartily as did my grandma. I immediately realised the significance. When my parents took my grandad's ashes onto the Bolehills to scatter them, a gust of wind blew them back into their faces, hair and clothes, as if to say I am still with you. I knew that story though. For Dad to be convinced that I had really spoken to Grandad I needed to be able to tell him something I knew nothing about.

Grandad thought for a moment and then went to a cupboard above a chair. He took down a few sheets of paper, tore them up and threw them on the fire, then held out his open hands. They were perfect. He told me, telepathically, that I must convey the message to BOTH of my parents. I realised at that point that although I had perceived my grandad speaking to me, in fact his lips had never moved and his communications were all by symbol and telepathy.

His urgent message for me now, was, "Grow Up!" At the same time he conveyed the concept telepathically that if you don't feel the love from your parents, or others, you aren't 'whole' and can't really grow up.

Grandma was so happy to be with Grandad at long last. They embraced and after a few moments Grandad turned to me and said, "And tell your father I didn't do enough of this!" I knew exactly what he meant. He hadn't shown my father enough affection.

It was then that I received a message in my head. "There is nothing to fear – but fear." I realised immediately that this was meant in two ways – there was nothing – no-thing – to fear – no substance to the notion of fear, as death is not as we know it, and that it is our fears that cause many of the problems here. On reflection I realised that this powerful message was from spirit world collectively. They were reassuring me that I was safe and had nothing to fear.

Because I felt safe, I just accepted my new reality, and was open to communication. I was shown golden bands of light that surrounded Earth like a grid. I was told about the changes that the planet Earth and humanity would undergo. And I was also told that I was here to work as part of a team.

With Grandad and Grandma more settled within me, I joined the rest of the group. Later in the afternoon there was no one more surprised than I, when during a group discussion, having heard a lady express her concerns about what was happening on the planet, I stood up (not seemingly moving my own body) and out of my mouth came the following words; "Don't be fearful of the changes, they are happening for humanity's highest good. Spirit world is well aware of the changes that are unfolding on the Earth plane and are doing what they can to assist at this time." Then I stopped talking and, realising that everyone was looking at me, quickly sat down. I don't think I've ever been so red-faced in all my life! But I also knew that what I'd said needed to be said.

I don't think anybody from the course, including the trainer, knew quite how to deal with me. They were, however, all incredibly supportive. A couple of the course participants had had something to do with the spiritual side of life, but nobody realised quite what was happening to me, and nor did I! Initially the trainer's explanation of 'parts' and 'inner child' had reassured me that what was happening to me was part of the NLP process and that everyone potentially was having similar experiences with the exercises. But after the experience with Grandad and Grandma and the messages that were clearly coming from another plane I began to realise that this was more than just NLP at work.

Grandma and Grandad stayed with me throughout the rest of the day. It was quite odd going home on the tube and then the train, with two spirit bodies inside of my physical body, chatting with them occasionally in my head. As we travelled, I noted in my diary the events of this interesting day.

As I got home and put the key in the lock of the door, thoughts raced through my mind. How was I going to tell my partner, Manos?

Manos was, and is, a very gentle soul, extremely kind and loving and very open. I felt sure he would understand, but where does one start to talk of experiences like this? I hadn't even heard or read about people having these kinds of experiences. I told him everything that had happened in the sequence it happened, and he listened. Truly listened. It was just what I needed at that time.

Manos didn't profess to understand what had happened to me, but he did believe me and that was really important. It gave me the strength to pick up the phone to pass on Grandad's message to the first of my parents.

My parents had separated when I was 18. My father had remarried and lived near Tadcaster, North Yorkshire where he and his wife ran a good old English pub. I took a few deep breaths and sat myself at the bottom of the stairs. It took a lot to pick up the phone to speak to my father. I told him what had happened to me. I told him how Grandad had stood on the chair and removed the papers from the top shelf of the cupboard. Dad confirmed that he did have a tall cupboard, and that on the top shelf of the cupboard he kept Grandad's certificates that he'd got working in a munitions factory. I felt confident now that the message was correct.

Then Dad asked me how Grandad's hands had appeared when he'd held them out to me. I said they were perfect hands and I suddenly realised that it could not have been Grandad because Grandad had the ends of two of his fingers missing. My heart sank. There was no point in continuing. I must have got it all wrong. I put the phone down feeling quite shocked and disappointed at what had happened. How could I have been so foolish? How could I have thought that I was really seeing my grandad? Grandad was dead. Was I going mad? Was this what it was like when you went mad? It had all seemed so real. It was real. Why didn't the message make sense? My confidence was shattered.

Something, I don't know what, still made me pick up the phone to my mother though, and when I told her what I'd seen, she had a completely different response. Throughout the difficulties in my mother and father's marriage, my grandad had appeared regularly to my mother in her dreams. She had told me about these dreams before but what she hadn't told me was that each time he appeared, he would show her his hands spread out in the same way I had described to her in my vision of him. His hands were always perfect. Mum suggested that this was to show that in the after life, all of our physical frailties or deformities are healed and we are perfect.

Grandad's actions were symbolic. The certificates were given to him when he worked at a munitions factory during the war. It was at the munitions factory he severed his fingers in an accident. In tearing up the certificates he was confirming that his injuries were healed and the certificates were no longer relevant. I didn't know about the certificates or the cupboard. I knew the ends of his fingers were missing but I had never known about the accident that had removed them until Dad told me that day. My mother and I were now both convinced that my experience had been an authentic communication from Grandad. I understood now, why my grandad had been so adamant that I had to convey the message to BOTH parents.

More pieces of the jigsaw became apparent when in subsequent years, my father confided that as my grandfather died, my father asked him from the deepest part of his heart and soul to look after me. We can only imagine that Grandad picked up on this heartfelt request and did exactly as my father had asked, staying with me, rather than making the transition.

Later that evening, as I lay in bed, I checked that Grandad and Grandma were still with me. They were, but not as strongly. And I now felt another presence. I felt a third, very loving light presence that felt very wise and clear and that made me feel safe.

As I lay on the bed I was given a further insight into my experiences. If as a child you don't have love to make you whole you create a protective skin or shield around yourself. To become whole and realise (real-ise as in make real) your full potential, you have to lose the skin, release the shield. But it is almost a Catch 22 situation. You created the skin to protect yourself and help yourself feel safe, but your creation of the skin or shield stops you from feeling the love that surrounds you, and so feeling safe.

We have to bring the defensive systems and shields we have in place into our conscious awareness to transcend them. Growing up is when we accept responsibility for our 'I' or for the personality-self we have created. We start seeing it for what it is; our creation, a collection of fears and desires, and we no longer allow it to determine our level of happiness or success, our experience of love or our experience of life.

It was time for me to GROW UP, to accept responsibility for my life, but I had no idea yet just what that would entail.

We are Not Alone

I vividly remember when I awoke the next morning, getting into the shower and having Grandad and Grandma with me, inside my body, while I was showering! It was such an odd experience! My mind wondered just how often spirit are with us when we are doing personal things! And as quickly as the thought came in, I dismissed it – it just wasn't important. What was important was that they were there, they were around us and that there was no death.

Grandad and Grandma travelled with me again on the train and then on the tube, in my body, just hugging each other like they would never, ever, let go again. I didn't know how long they were going to be with me for. I was just really enjoying the experience of having them with me.

When I arrived at Regent's College, I joined the others for morning coffee. Although I still had Grandma and Grandad with me, I was otherwise entirely back to 'normal'! I felt more in control of the situation. I had become used to the idea that there was some sort of life after death and of my grandparents being actually with me in my body.

When the course was about to start we all entered the main room. It was a beautiful morning and sun streamed in through the large windows on two sides of the room. Immediately I became aware of noise in my head and figures around the room, figures that looked much like you or I, although they appeared less dense in substance. It was as though I would be able to put my hand right through them if I tried. The figures were in full colour and looked very much like a reflection in glass. Their feet hovered slightly off the floor, and in a room of sixty-four physical people, I would say there were also about another two hundred of these 'spirit' type forms.

After feeling more in control earlier I was now feeling confused and deeply shocked at this bizarre turn of events. My heart raced and with it my thoughts. Had someone drugged me? Had someone put something in the coffee or the biscuits we had on arrival? Having never experimented with drugs, I wondered if this was what happened when you did. Was this what hallucinating was like? Thoughts of madness rushed through my mind again. My logical brain was struggling to make sense of what was happening. They didn't look like Grandad had; he had been much smaller and a vivid image in my body and so it didn't occur to me straight away that what I was seeing was 'dead' people.

I sat very still. I felt sure it would wear off soon.

The first break was more than an hour away. I tried hard to focus on what the trainer was saying, but failed dismally. My attention kept being pulled back to the floating figures in the room.

Seeing the floating figures was less frightening than hearing all their voices shouting at me in my head. It started to distress me. I didn't know what to do. I hoped the noise would stop soon. It didn't. It got stronger. In what seemed like no time at all I was frozen to my chair. I couldn't hear myself think – literally. So many voices were shouting at me. I wanted to shut them out. I wanted my own thoughts in my head, not theirs.

Reflecting on the experience some time later I realised that they were not shouting at me because they were angry. They were shouting because they desperately wanted to get through and get a message to their loved ones. What they didn't realise though was that if they all shouted at once I couldn't hear what any one of them was saying. I often wonder now, how many of the people society classes as mentally ill are just extremely psychic and not aware of how to control or develop it. How many such people are on medications that simply create another set of problems for them? I feel sure that having developed my left-brain, the logical rational side, that this actually stood me in good stead and helped me keep my feet on the ground through this time.

A lady came over to me at the first break and said, "Look, I can see you're in distress. What's wrong?" I told her what was happening to me.

She said, "Try surrounding yourself with light." I wanted to laugh at her suggestion but managed instead to say, "What do you mean?"

"Use your imagination and surround yourself with light. That will protect you."

I thought, "What? I'm hearing voices and seeing things and she thinks that surrounding myself with light is going to make a difference?" I didn't have a better idea though. This was completely new territory for me. The noise remained totally unbearable, so I did as she suggested.

It was difficult at first, because I truly didn't have much of an imagination. As a child, I was encouraged to study maths and sciences. I had a very good brain, a very good memory and a very good way of organising information within my brain and retrieving it in exam situations. But I was not used to using my imagination. This was a new experience for me! I tried, however, using the same sort of process as the course leader had used when helping me to experience 'joy'. I put white light around me and a blob of blue on top of my head.

Why the blob of blue? I do not know to this day! But it worked. I could no longer hear or see the room full of spirits, with one exception.

A small child, who I initially thought was a little boy, was still making a noise in my head. This child wanted to speak to its father who was in the room. I knew from the telepathic image that was conveyed to me that the father had a certain style of hair, a beard and a moustache.

There were two men in the room to choose from who fitted this description. I focused on one, and then the other, but I couldn't work out which person this child wanted me to speak to. The child was using me as a messenger. After a while, I stopped trying. The child was getting increasingly frustrated, and so was I. My head was starting to hurt. As soon as I stopped trying I knew exactly which man I had to go to. At the next break I went over to him and said, "I don't understand what's happening to me right now, but I've been seeing a small child, and the child wants to talk to you." It was common knowledge that I was having strange experiences but he didn't know what exactly I had been going through. I felt he was humouring me but he agreed to help me if he could.

We went to a quiet room and I established a link with the child. Water was pouring down my arms; it was more than just sweat. I had never had that happen to me before. The room was not hot. I didn't understand why water should be literally running down my arms. I was compelled to pass on a message. It was really, really hard work and very emotional. It was out of my control. The child, no more than three or four, showed me the inside of the house where they used to live, and the gentleman confirmed that the layout I described was correct. The child also showed me a silver bike. The bike was very special to the child. That was about as much as I could bring through. It took huge amounts of energy and concentration. The gentleman thanked me for what I'd done, but admitted he didn't really understand what the message was about. I wondered why he couldn't connect with what I was saying because the images were so clear.

A year later, when I met his wife, I learned that the child I was seeing was a girl, his daughter who had passed over at the age of four. Had I told him that it was a little girl, he may have been more receptive to the message and made the connection.

That particular day Jane, a trained spiritual healer who happened to be on the course gave me a book. It was a small green book called, 'Seven Steps to Eternity,' by a gentleman called Stephen Turoff. As she gave me the book Jane said, "I don't really understand what's happening to you, but I feel this book will help. I felt I had to bring it for you today." The book was just what I needed. It talked about seven levels of existence, or seven kingdoms or heavens that exist, and somehow that felt correct for me. It was as though I was reading about what I already knew on some level. One chapter talked about the fear that animals go through before they are slaughtered. How fear is a vibration and how when we then eat the flesh of the animal we also ingest their fear. It is very difficult for us as human beings to process the animals' fear. That too, felt so obvious and correct that I decided there and then to become a vegetarian and have remained so ever since, though I do not believe that everyone should become a vegetarian. I think we should each listen to what our bodies tell us.

After the course finished that day, some of the group headed for the local bar. I thought it would do me good to join the group and perhaps take my mind off things. One thing I really liked about the course was how friendly everyone was. Once there, I joined a group that I hadn't really got to know so far. In no time at all I was feeling part of the group and they were explaining to me all about something they called, 'love energy'.

A dark-haired young girl called Sarah Jane was the youngest member of the group. I sensed that she was part of the learning I was experiencing. With hindsight I consider she was an advanced soul. She explained how you could build this love energy up within you and then send it to another person, almost as a ball and they would feel it hit them. She demonstrated by sending a ball of energy over to one of the young men. I didn't know what she was talking about. So she created another ball within her and then touched me on my shoulder. Warm tingling energy moved from my shoulder into the middle of my chest; what I now know as my 'heart centre'. It was as though my whole chest opened up, spilling warmth and tingling into the whole of my being. It was an awesome feeling. I felt like I was floating, filled with love, filled with light! I floated onto the tube that night. In fact, I floated all the way home! And the next day, I was still floating.

I was thoroughly enjoying the course and I was very glad that it did require me to concentrate and join in so much. It helped keep me in the 'here and now' and prevented me dwelling too much on the changes I was experiencing in my life. In fact, I was so focused, I did not even notice Grandma and Grandad leave. I don't remember them saying goodbye or departing, as such, at all. I began to sense them less strongly within me after seeing all the other spirits and they gradually withdrew though I have experienced them with me on a great many other occasions since.

Life returned to some kind of normality until another evening at the bar. A lady who I hadn't had much to do with on the course came over and asked to talk with me. She said she was particularly interested in what was happening to me, because her sister was dying of cancer and my experiences had given her new hope. She asked me if it was possible for me to give her some kind of proof. She didn't specify what kind of proof, but at the same time I instinctively knew that I would like to help her if I could. I said I'd do my best, and internally I made the request that this lady be given her proof she needed. Word had obviously got around that I was seeing spirits.

As things turned out, we didn't have to wait very long; about a couple of hours. The two of us travelled home on the same tube, sitting together, sharing our thoughts, and talking about the events of the day. As we travelled I was vaguely aware of an elderly white-haired man with vivid blue eyes, sitting diagonally across from me, looking at me. I ignored his gaze and continued talking with my new friend. I was sure I didn't know him, but perhaps he thought he knew me.

When the tube came to a stop, the man with white hair rose and stood in the aisle with his arm stretched outwards, as if waiting for us to get up, but we weren't getting off the tube at that stop, so we stayed talking. The gentleman continued to stand there, and the tube continued to remain stationary in the station. This went on for a while. After a few minutes, we both turned around to see where the tube had stopped. It had stopped at a station that was not on our normal route. We couldn't understand why that should be, and decided we had better investigate.

The tube had stopped at its terminus. Somehow, we had both managed to get on the wrong tube although we had each taken the same correct tube independently every night for several nights previously. How could we both have got on the wrong tube? It didn't make sense!

We quickly got off the tube. On the platform, the man with white hair and vivid blue eyes was waiting for us. He was an elderly man with a stocky build, an inch or so smaller than me. He had an open friendly face, thick pure white hair and the most amazing cobalt blue eyes I had ever seen. I had never seen eyes like his in my life.

"I bet I know what you do," he said. And thinking I was humouring a sweet, old man, I said, "Yes, go on then!"

"You are here as a healer and a teacher," he said.

"Well, yes, sort of," I said, again humouring him. "I work for a bank. I'm a training manager. I dare say you could call that teaching." He looked directly at me with those vivid blue eyes and said, "Don't forget the ones that can't see. The ones that can't see can still feel the vibration." He tapped his right foot with his walking stick to reinforce the point.

I smiled at him, thinking in my head, "What on earth is this guy on about!" He turned to leave, and my friend and I turned away to look at the information screen to work out which tube we needed to catch to get ourselves back to our correct line. When we looked back to where the old man had been, he was already on the upward escalator. At the exact same moment we looked at each other. I said, "Are you thinking what I'm thinking?" She nodded and said, "He isn't of this earth!" I don't know how, but we just knew inside that he wasn't like us. I ran to catch him up. He wouldn't turn to face me again. He just lifted his left hand and said, "Good luck! Good luck!"

Meeting that man was the proof that my friend had wanted. She was in tears. He'd had a profound effect on us both. My mind was racing and my heart was pounding. Who was he? What was he? What did he mean? Why would I need good luck? Why would he not turn to face me again? With those eyes, those amazing eyes – why hadn't I realised he was different sooner? Was he a guide? Was he a guide sent to help on this journey I had embarked on? The experience was what we had both needed. There seemed nothing more to say.

By the time we got back on the right tube, and I got onto my train to Haslemere, I'd given up thinking about it, because there weren't any apparent answers and my head was starting to ache. I opened a book I was reading and the very next paragraph in the book read, 'A seventh level Master/Teacher/Guide has access to all the dimensions and can manifest physically on the earth plane . . .' The hairs on my arms stood on end and I absolutely knew that I had met a Master/Teacher from the Seventh Dimension.

So many times I reflected on what the blue-eyed man's message meant. I was here as a teacher and a healer and I was not to forget the ones that cannot see as they can still feel the vibration! I knew what a teacher was and I was a trainer not a teacher. I did not want to be a teacher. I wanted to work with adults, empowering adults. I didn't believe I was here as a teacher. I liked children but I didn't think teaching was my forte.

I knew what a healer was but I had no known abilities there. Don't forget the ones that cannot see – did he mean I would be working with blind people? Vibration; was that something musical? Would I be doing something musical with blind children? It didn't make sense, and why would I need luck?

It would take me a long time to unravel what he said, but once I did, it made perfect sense.

A Purpose

It was the following Friday that I experienced more teaching, if I can call it that, and another very peculiar phenomenon. The course had finished and the group was going to the pub. I needed some cash, so I headed to the cash dispenser first. It was just a few minutes walk from the college.

After getting the cash I needed, I passed a man who was begging and who clearly had an alcohol problem. He was dirty, smelly and not quite with us. I gave him ten pounds. I thought it was the right thing to do. A lump formed in my stomach. An insight formed in my mind. "This is partly where we have gone wrong. We should be giving each other love rather than money." came the insight. Giving the beggar money was the easy option. It would have been so much more difficult and yet powerful to show the man compassion by giving him a hug. I felt tears welling in my eyes. It hadn't entered my head to hug him. I had only thought of money as the solution. I was ashamed.

Instead of going to the pub I decided to go home, so I made my way to the tube. But when I got to the entrance of the tube station, I couldn't go through it. I physically walked into what felt like a force field. I couldn't see anything, but I couldn't pass through the entrance that, seemingly, had nothing in it but air. Other people walked past me into the station on either side; only I could not pass. I worried about what I must look like taking one step forward and then bouncing backwards. At the same time, I was drawn to go back to the park that surrounded Regent's College. I decided not to embarrass myself any further and headed back to the park.

I had to walk past the pub where some of my colleagues were still socialising to get to the park. I desperately hoped they would not see me but they did and called out to me to join them. I shouted back that I had to go to the park. I hoped that they would understand and wouldn't follow me. I really didn't want to appear any stranger to them than I already did.

The park was relatively quiet. It was a lovely summer's evening and I was amazed that there were so few visitors to the park. I found myself a quiet spot not far from the entrance, facing the lake, and sat down on the grass. I took out my notebook and noted my experiences. What was happening to me? The force field, or whatever it was stopping me getting onto the tube, was like something out of Star Trek. It sounded so far-fetched to me, even though I had experienced it exactly as I describe. Seeing dead people was bad enough but invisible force fields? I decided to keep this one to myself.

I wrote about the incident with the beggar and other events from the day. Over an hour passed, and I started to become conscious that if I didn't meet whoever I was to meet, or see whatever it was I needed to see soon, I would miss my last train home.

I got out my train timetable and, sure enough, only about forty-five minutes remained spare if I was to catch the tube and then my train. More to myself than anyone else, I said, "Look, I'm happy to sit here and experience whatever it is I need to experience, but can you please hurry up, because I do need to go home?"

I didn't have to wait very long. Two women came along pushing babies in buggies and they asked me for money. They were quite poorly dressed and seemed genuinely in need of money. I felt that they would use it wisely and not squander it, as the man earlier would have done so I gave them five pounds. I figured that, if they needed to ask, then they probably really needed the money far more than I did.

A few moments later, a young girl of nine or ten came along, pushing a further buggy, and it was clear that she was with the first two ladies who had gone ahead. She, too, asked for money, saying she was hungry. I said, "I've just given some to your mum."

"That's not my mum," she snapped, and I knew for certain that she was not telling the truth.

Then I noticed that there were three children. There was the girl who was pushing the buggy, who was nine or ten years old. There was a baby of probably two years of age, in the buggy. Then there was a smaller boy of probably four years of age, to one side of the buggy. All looked as though they could do with a bath.

I looked inside my purse and there were three one-pound coins, one coin for each child. I gave one coin to the sleeping child in the buggy. I sensed that his 'light' was still on internally. I gave another coin to the small boy beside the buggy. As I gave him the coin, I knew also, that his 'light' was still on, but possibly not for much longer. And I gave the third coin to the girl, but I couldn't detect a 'light' within her.

As I gave the coins I found myself saying, "This comes with love for the goodness inside you." As I said the words to the boy his face lit up. He knew what I meant. As soon as they moved away from me, I saw the girl snatch the two one-pound coins off her younger brothers. For the older girl, the money was all important. For the younger boy it was the expression of love. At that moment I knew absolutely, that I was here to help children keep their 'lights' on.

I wasn't sure exactly what that meant but I have since come to believe that what I describe here as their 'lights' may also be described as their 'Divine spark', the 'God consciousness' that exists within each and every one of us. The negativity and materialism of this dimension can easily cause us to lose our connection with the 'Divine', with God, with nature, with life, unless we remain conscious of these things and work at preserving them.

I felt that having experienced these events and insights, my work in the park was finished so I made my way back to the tube. I walked through the entrance without difficulty this time. I was relieved, as I was getting rather tired and needed to get home.

I had come to welcome my train journeys now and even look forward to them. They gave me time to reflect on my experiences and write about what I was learning. The journeys passed quickly rather than dragging and the dirty windows just didn't bother me at all any more. I was oblivious to them. I threw myself into the course each day. I was learning so much about myself and about others. A big part of the course was learning that, to a greater or lesser extent, we all have similar fears and that inside we all basically want the same kinds of things. We all express those fears, wants and needs in different ways.

One of the exercises I found most inspiring was one where we each worked out what we really wanted from our lives. The whole process took about a day and a half with many smaller exercises leading up to the final goal. What did I really want to achieve this lifetime? I realised that I wanted to, 'dream incredible dreams and manifest them'. Part of this dream would be the establishment of a 'Dream Foundation' where people who had good business ideas that would benefit humanity could gain funds to get their projects off the ground. This in turn would help many others along with me to be fulfilled and peaceful and would be my way of contributing to world peace.

The whole realisation, as significant as it was, was secondary to seeing what everyone else on the course wanted to achieve. All of us had worked independently or perhaps used one other person as a sounding board. Each individual gave a presentation describing what they wanted to achieve. It took the best part of a day. Every one of the sixty-four presentations was inspired by or spoke of a higher need to contribute to creating a peaceful world. I could feel a lump in my throat; I was not the only one. Some people cried openly. For the first time in my life the prospect of world peace suddenly seemed like an achievable possibility.

Each day, at the conclusion of the training, we all had lots to talk about and process. Going to the bar after the course became a regular and important event; almost integral to the course. One evening, the course trainer came across to me in the bar. We sat at a table near a window, so we had some privacy. He wanted to talk about what I had been experiencing. As we talked it became clear that my initial feelings, that this was more than just NLP at work were verified. He was interested in the impact his course was having on me. He had thought that I was undergoing a normal progression but it had now gone way beyond that and he was curious about what I was experiencing.

He asked me lots of questions about my experiences, and I answered them as truthfully as I could, even though I did not fully understand either. At the end of our discussion he turned to me and said that as far as he could detect, using his skills with NLP, I was telling the truth. All my body language and my eye movements were consistent with somebody who believed their experiences. But nevertheless, my beliefs about what I had experienced didn't fit his view of the world. He couldn't offer any explanations for the strange phenomena I had experienced and neither could I.

For some reason I found myself saying, "I am here to give people proof." Immediately I wondered where on earth those words had come from! He immediately took me up on this and said the proof he wanted was to see me 'walk on water'. I don't know why, but in that moment of time, 'walking on water' seemed like it was absolutely possible. Though it seems crazy now,

I felt an overwhelming conviction that I could provide proof in any way he wanted. And so we went down to the lake at Regent's Park and I stood close to the water's edge with the trainer. The confidence I had felt moments earlier seeped away as my rational thoughts took over. In a highly enhanced state I felt I should be able to walk on water, but I was afraid to do so because all of my experiences of the physical laws of this world kept reinforcing that we can't walk on water.

I didn't really know what to do. I must have stayed there for a good ten minutes, so in desperation I internally asked for help, asked for guidance, asked for the gentleman with the white hair and blue eyes to appear. Nothing happened. It was a summer's evening, and although the weather was mild, I was starting to get very cold in my lightweight, summer dress. I started to shiver and the trainer put his jacket around me. Again I stood there praying for help as hard as I knew how and nothing happened. Nothing. I was cold and tired. Eventually I decided to swallow my pride. I gave in and shook my head. "I can't do it." I admitted and we both silently headed back to the bar. I was so embarrassed; I didn't know what to say. I was disappointed and angry too. What were these messages that I was getting? And why wasn't I able to fulfil them? The trainer must surely have thought I was going mad.

Back at the bar, I picked up my things and made my way back to the tube, internally severely reprimanding my guides, or whoever it was that was working with me, for not helping me out. "What are you doing setting me up like this? How can you say, out of my mouth, that I'm here to give people proof, and then not allow me to give them the proof that they want? What is going on?" I demanded to see the man with the white hair and blue eyes.

I got onto the tube and the feelings of embarrassment continued to flood my mind. I was distraught. What must my trainer think of me? I felt sure I must sound like I was losing it. Would he still want me on the course? How would I explain to my employer if I were sent home from the course? As I stepped off the tube I noticed a blind man with dark glasses and a white stick. I laughed internally. "I know I'm a beginner," I said, "but you're sending me a blind 'guide'? And now, when it's too late?"

I wondered if the man's eyes would be vivid blue like the last guide and if that was why he was wearing dark glasses. I decided that I wasn't going to make it easy for him whoever he was. I wanted to be sure that my request for a guide had been answered and test him, so I deliberately set off down a different tunnel. I could not believe it when within a few paces I walked straight into him. He stood in front of me with his arms outstretched! I couldn't possibly miss him. I wasn't meant to.

He introduced himself and asked me to help him catch his train. I had spent so much time at the lake, I would only have enough time to help this 'man' to his train, and then catch my own last train. He asked me if I had made my decision yet, and I presumed he was asking me if I accepted the purpose the man with blue eyes and white hair had spoken of; that I was here as a teacher and healer. He hoped I would make the right decision. "Do you know what to do for the best?" he asked.

"I know exactly what to do for the best, but I don't know how or what it will entail," I responded. He just nodded.

The man told me that his name was Liam. As I had expected, there was just enough time to get him onto his train before I literally had to run for my own. There wasn't the opportunity for me to ask any more questions.

My head was in complete turmoil now. Another bizarre encounter. Thinking I could walk on water! Thoughts were racing through my mind. Who am I? Who are these two 'men' if that is what they are? Why did they talk to me? Why did they talk about my purpose and responsibility? What on earth is going on? The train journey passed too quickly for me this time. I still needed time and space to work this all out. Why did they not appear with me at the lake? Why did I have to bear all this by myself?

I knew I needed help, but I didn't know where to turn for that help. I stopped at a local church on the way home – just in case there was someone there to help me. I found its doors closed, but then it was late at night. Where did people go when they had experiences like this? Was I the only one or did people just not talk about this kind of thing? By the time I got home I was quite a mess, and my partner, Manos, was concerned about me. When I'd come home with Grandad and Grandma that was different. I'd been very happy, very calm, very in charge of things. But now he was seeing a different side of things. I was totally confused and very upset. I wanted to know what was happening to me. And I didn't know where to turn for help.

We sat talking into the night. I told Manos all about the experience with the trainer. How could I ever even think about walking on the lake at Regent's Park! We both laughed! Maybe Manos too, thought I was going mad, but if he did, he kindly kept that thought to himself. It was a difficult time for me and probably even harder for Manos because he wasn't a part of my experiences. He only had my word for what had happened and I knew how far-fetched it all sounded.

I half expected him to phone for a doctor and get me psychiatrically assessed. Thankfully, he didn't.

My head felt like it was ready to explode. It hurt from thinking about things and trying to analyse what was happening to me. Where was it all taking me? If I wasn't already mad, a few more days like this and I soon would be. I was so glad that the next day was Sunday. The course ran from Monday to Saturday inclusive and I was so thankful that tomorrow I would have a day off.

It took a while for my mind to relax that night. Sleep, when it finally did come, was a welcome relief.

I could not go on like this.

Looking for Answers

Overnight, I came up with the idea of contacting Stephen Turoff, the author of the book 'Seven Steps to Eternity', because all the knowledge and information in that book seemed so well to match my own inner-knowing.

Now, what were the chances of finding the author of the book? Stephen Turoff's address and telephone number weren't printed in the book. All I had to go on was the author's name. And to make matters worse, the book was privately printed, so I couldn't even contact the publishers and go through them. The only thing I could think of was to ring Jane, the lady who had given me the book. It was a long shot, but I was desperate.

I searched for her number in my course notes. I prayed that she would be able to help and that she hadn't gone out for the day. Jane answered immediately and to my amazement, she did know the author's phone number and address as she had met him once.

Stephen Turoff had a healing centre in Banbury. Jane gave me the telephone number and wished me luck in getting to see him.

Since I'd previously worked in Oxford, I knew the area of Banbury quite well, so I phoned to see if I could make an appointment to see the author. The receptionist told me, "I'm sorry, Mr Turoff has a waiting list of about three months." Now I knew why Jane had wished me luck. "Oh, wait a minute, there is one cancellation at twelve o'clock tomorrow," the receptionist suddenly corrected herself. I checked with Manos and he said, "Yes, we'll go." He really appreciated how desperate I was for help at this time. It would mean missing a day of the course but I really needed someone to help me understand what was happening to me. The receptionist gave me the address of the healing centre and directions to find it.

When I came off the phone, Manos looked at the address and the directions. He laughed. "That's not Banbury, that's Danbury. Banbury is in Oxfordshire, Danbury is in Chelmsford in Essex. It's a totally different place." He said it in a manner that suggested that it would not be possible or sensible to travel that far for such a purpose. Danbury was much further away. I really needed to go, however, and I couldn't hide the disappointment in my voice. "I have made the appointment now," I said. "I really do need to go." Manos nodded in acceptance and agreement. He had been my partner for over two years and had never seen me like this before. He was as out of his own depth as I was out of mine.

"Yes,' he said thoughtfully. "We'll go then."

I could hardly sleep that night. I felt sure Stephen would have the answers I was looking for, or at least be able to point me in the right direction.

It was a long journey to Danbury, almost 3 hours, and then we had difficulty finding the healing centre itself as it was not visible from the main road and was tucked in behind a hotel. By the time we pulled up outside, just ten minutes remained before my appointment was due. I was so glad we had allowed extra time for the journey. The car park was brimming with cars. It seemed there were far too many cars there for the size of the healing centre and this was confirmed when we opened the door. The room and the adjacent hallway were filled with Indian families. Incense hung heavily in the air. As we squeezed our way through into the waiting area, trying not to bump into people, I noticed there were lots of pictures on the wall of a man with an afro-style hair, and wearing a bright orange robe. I wondered who he was. There was what I could only describe as a simple shrine in the corner of the room, with photographs of people who'd requested healing, or rather, whose families had requested healing for them. Indian music was playing, and Manos and I looked at each other sceptically. We hadn't expected this. We kept our heads down, and felt really uncomfortable. What had we come to?

Stephen Turoff as it turned out, was, and is, a renowned psychic surgeon. On the wall there were several photographs of him with his hands above different patients. Each had at least one beam of coloured light coming into the area where he was working. Stephen had an incredible list of healing miracles attributed to him by his patients, but did not profess to offer miracle cures himself. The long waiting list and the daily queues at his clinic spoke volumes for his abilities. His average time with a client was apparently less than ten minutes and yet seemingly he was getting excellent results.

We must have waited for about half an hour but it felt like much longer until eventually my name was called. The receptionist explained to us that Stephen often worked in a trance, so if he seemed odd with us in any way and talked in a funny voice, an Austrian accent, this was just his guide 'a deceased medical doctor' working through him. It all sounded rather weird and did not make us feel any more comfortable. You may be able to imagine how uneasy we felt by this stage but I had to go through with it because I needed to better understand what it was I was experiencing. I hoped he would be able to help.

Stephen had two rooms in which he saw people. This arrangement enabled him to see as many people as possible in as short a time as possible. We were settled into one room while he was treating another client in an adjacent room. We waited, wondering quite what we would experience. We didn't have to wait long. When Stephen came in, it was clear he was in an altered state. He was an impressive-looking man, at over 6 feet tall and dressed in a white coat and open sandals. Stephen asked me to sit on the examination table and I did as instructed. Before I had time to even think he had his large hands on my neck and quickly manipulated my neck causing it to crack loudly. It wasn't painful at all but the crack took me by surprise. I hadn't realised that there was anything 'wrong' with my neck but it felt much easier after the manipulation. What would happen next? I glanced over to Manos who was sitting in the corner of the room a few feet away. I had so many questions but didn't dare voice them.

Stephen, or rather the spirit that was in Stephen's body, looked me straight in the eye and said, "The Christ is already on the earth and has ten million followers. His name is Sai Baba and he lives in India. When you know that you are God, when you know that all is God, only then, you will be able to step out of the boat and onto the water.

Find God.

There is only God.

All is God. See God in all. Everything you see, see it as God, even the air around you. All is God.

All else is illusion.

Meditate.

You had a bad experience when you were three but you came through it."

That was all he said, and he left the room. But in that brief exchange, he'd addressed my two main concerns and helped me greatly in the process.

Going home in the car, I reflected on my experience with Stephen. He had said that I'd had a bad experience when I was three and that was absolutely correct. I had come very close to drowning in an algae-covered pond that I had stepped onto, not knowing that it was water. With that observation, he had confirmed for me, that he, or the 'spirit' that was with him, knew things about me that were not well-known and that he couldn't have known. This was important because it gave the rest of his message credibility.

However, most important were his other comments. Only Manos, the trainer and I knew about my experience by the water's edge at Regent's Park and yet Stephen Turoff had talked about 'walking on water'. Although he hadn't said a lot to me, he'd said what I needed to hear. He had affirmed that some higher consciousness knew about the incident at the park and that something out of the ordinary was happening to me. It was real; I wasn't just making it up or imagining it.

After the 'walking on water' incident, I'd had worrying thoughts going through my mind about my mental state. I hadn't even shared these concerns with Manos. I had begun to wonder whether I thought I was a 'Christ'. I had a very limited knowledge of mental health but I did know that thinking you're a 'Christ' was one sign of schizophrenia. I felt sure I was still sane. If I was insane, surely I would not still be trying to reason and work everything out like this. Stephen had reassured me that I was not a 'Christ' and not crazy. His message left me with a sense of peace.

At the time, I couldn't have told you the name of the 'Christ' that he told me was on the earth, but I knew that I'd recognise the face, the afro hair and the orange robe if I ever saw them again.

Manos and I returned home. It had been a strange and tiring day. We talked about how uncomfortable we had felt in the healing centre and about Stephen's incredible popularity with Indian families. The photographs of Stephen healing had impressed us both. There were far too many of them with beams of light clearly visible across them to be explained rationally. We wondered what the real Stephen was like when he wasn't in a trance. I wondered if he would like an apprentice. I would love to be able to do what he did, I thought, although I kept that thought to myself as there had been enough weirdness for one day.

By the time we returned home I was much more at peace with myself than I had been. I was still thoroughly bemused by what was happening to me but felt very much that I was being 'looked after'. I was confident that I could return to the course the next day and get back into the NLP.

The remainder of the course passed relatively uneventfully. The end of the five weeks came all too quickly and we were all sorry to have to part and return to our positions. We exchanged phone numbers and promised to keep in touch.

I had a weekend at home before I was due to return to the bank on the Monday morning. Manos was working that Saturday and it was good to have some time just for me. I didn't feel right inside. There was a vague uneasiness within me. Before the NLP course I would not have paid attention to it. I would have just got on with something – washing, ironing or whatever. Now I knew I needed to pay attention to my feelings. What was it? Why was I so uneasy? The answer came easily enough. Work! I was worried about going back to work. All through the past few weeks the 'safe' environment of the course had protected me from feeling too threatened. People were friendly and non-judgemental. What would it be like back at work where the people would be sure to notice the change in me?

I started to think through my experiences. Although the visit to Stephen had been helpful in many regards, I hadn't been able to talk to him. I desperately needed someone to talk to and to help me make sense of it all. What if I continued to see 'dead people' when I returned to work? I knew my experiences sounded bizarre. What if, as a worst-case scenario, word came back from someone else attending the course about what had happened to me? I would very likely be suspended pending psychiatric assessment. How would that look? I would be lucky to get another job; it would be the end of my career.

Prior to my experiences I had always been very sceptical of people who called themselves 'psychic' or 'clairvoyant'. I considered that most people, if they went to see a psychic, would be going for a relationship issue or something to do with work, health or financial matters. My rational mind had decided that psychics probably worked by looking carefully at a person, observing their body language while making general statements and then leading the conversation in a way that told the client what they wished to hear. I certainly didn't consider they were 'real'. I knew from my time in lending for example that often by looking carefully at someone, you could guess what they did for a living and what it was they had come in to the bank for.

Recently, however, I had accepted that there might well be more to this psychic business than I had previously thought. And I now felt that talking with a psychic person might actually be a good idea. I reasoned though that it would have to be someone who was reputable and personally recommended. I remembered that Jennifer, the lady who had first helped me talk to Grandad, had mentioned to me that if ever I needed help or needed someone to talk to there was a psychic lady she had heard very good reports about. I had written the name of the lady in my course notes more out of politeness than with any real intention of phoning her. Now I knew that I needed to get in touch with her.

I flicked through my course notes to find the phone number. Why did I always take such extensive notes? I couldn't find it. My search became more frantic. I knew I had definitely written it down somewhere. At last I found it.

The lady's name was Alison Harper. She was a clairvoyant and an astrologer and she worked from a practice in Croydon. I phoned her. I was very careful what I said to her, as I didn't want to give anything away. I wanted to make sure that I could feel that anything she said was credible, just as I had with

Stephen. She asked for my date of birth, time of birth and place of birth and that's all I gave her. She said to call her back in fifteen minutes, as she would need to call some astrological information up on her computer. It was a long fifteen minutes.

When I called her back, her first words to me were, "Oh! My dear, do you know that you're incredibly psychic and what's been happening to you over the past few weeks is that it's all been opening up." Remember, I had said nothing about what had been happening to me and yet she knew. You can imagine how I felt. I was gob-smacked! Totally gob-smacked! I was crying, partly from shock and partly with relief. I had found someone who once again had confirmed I wasn't going mad. That terrible fear I had kept pushing to the back of my mind since the experiences had started was at last being laid to rest. And she couldn't be reading my body language I reasoned as I was on the other end of a phone!

As if that was not enough, Alison went on. She talked about how hard Manos was finding the whole experience and the difficulties I would face when I returned to work. I was concerned about seeing spirits around people as I was working. Alison assured me that I was very well looked after and that everything was going according to plan. All I needed to do was trust my feelings. I was going to meet some pretty strange people along the way and would need to be able to sort the 'wheat from the chaff'. If I wanted to refine my abilities I was welcome to attend a development meeting that her group ran. In thirty minutes Alison somehow managed to allay all my fears. She explained that I was here as an ambassador. She assured me that my experience as a bank manager was going to stand me in good stead in terms of being taken seriously when I did more spiritual work and that I should not worry about things.

Alison said my astrological chart was amazing and that astrologically it was the time for this psychic ability to open up. She told me that there was a split in my career house and I would be going from one extreme of work – left-brain, logical, analytical – to the other extreme – right-brain, intuitive, creative. She said I was extraordinarily gifted as a psychic and would help a great many people. If I could help anyone as much as she helped me that afternoon I would be extremely grateful. I don't think she realised quite how accurate she was or how much her reading helped me at that time.

Alison sent me a tape of the reading, which I played again and again. It helped me through so many times when I worried about what was happening to me. It helped me keep my sanity when my life as I had known it, seemed to be disintegrating around me. I looked forward to eventually meeting her face-to-face one day. It would be a few months but that day would come.

A Choice to Make

Returning to work was very odd. I was still the same person inside, but now I knew there was no death and I could see, sense and hear loved ones around those I worked with. I was unsure when I should speak up and when I should keep what I knew to myself.

One noticeable effect of all my experiences so far, was that I no longer had any fear of dying. I had never really thought I had a fear of dying, but once you know that death is not final then it does totally change your perspective. When you lose your fear of death you lose a lot of other fears too. Having been through so much, I was no longer so concerned about what people thought of me and I no longer had Grandad with me holding me back. I was a changed person.

I made many mistakes with people as I learnt to live with the new me. People love you when you tell them something they want to hear, but they often attack you when you tell them something they don't want to hear.

With so much information about people available to me, I had to learn how to discern what to pass on and what to withhold. It was a difficult time for me and for those around me. There was much I needed to learn. I found myself living in two worlds; the rational banking world I had previously known and in which I had felt safe and successful, and now also a separate, private world in my head.

As I have said, I made many mistakes by sharing too much with the wrong people. My basic nature is very open and honest, sometimes to the point of complete tactlessness. In that respect I am a typical Sagittarian. The hardest person I had to deal with was my new line manager. We had only met a couple of weeks before I attended the NLP course and he had been dubious about the need for me to attend it at all. My basic desire to be honest meant that on returning I told him the truth about what had happened and that I could now see dead people. You might well imagine how that went down. His face was a picture. It wasn't what he wanted to hear at all. He didn't want me to talk to any of my colleagues about my experiences, which I didn't feel was fair. Some of my work colleagues were friends and I felt that I needed to talk with them socially about what I was experiencing. I felt that what I talked about with my friends was my business. So I ignored his direction.

Unfortunately, my relationship with my line manager became very strained, not just because of my psychic abilities but also because I operated from a place of possibility; I was now fascinated by what was possible. He operated from a place of necessity; he was interested in what was necessary to continue the work of the bank, as he had known it over time. I am sure he wasn't a bad manager; just struggling to know how to handle someone like me. This world-view mismatch meant that in his eyes I soon began to be regarded as a loose canon. In my eyes, he lacked vision. Unfortunately for me, he was the boss.

The only thing that made work bearable was the knowledge that he was based in Birmingham and I was based in Leeds. We had very little contact. I kept out of his way as much as I could and with hindsight he probably kept out of mine too. But it still was not a healthy working relationship.

I often wondered if it would have been any different had he known me before my experiences. Perhaps if I had first had the opportunity to earn his respect he would have been more tolerant of my new truth. Sadly, that had not been the case and he took me as he found me, as someone whose behaviour and thoughts were totally unexplainable in his terms.

Many of my colleagues were incredibly curious and very supportive. They wanted to know all about my experiences; how it had all started, what had happened, who they had with them and whether they could learn to see their loved ones too. The spiritual side of life soon became the main topic of conversation at lunchtime and after work. We didn't have many answers, but we had lots of questions, which is what happens when we wake up spiritually. We don't just wake up spiritually in isolation, those around us start to awaken too, or we intensify their internal fears as happened with my line manager. Sometimes though, there is a time delay and it can be quite lonely for a while. We can feel that no one understands us, including ourselves. For this reason having a group of like-minded people to share your experiences with can be very beneficial.

Although my work colleagues were fascinated, I didn't have anyone psychic to talk to and at times it seemed like no one really understood. I didn't feel I could keep phoning Alison Harper so I kept my thoughts in a diary and got my answers by going within. With hindsight, that was actually the best way forward but it took effort and discipline. It would have been so much easier just to ask someone else for the answers. I guess I had to learn the hard way!

I had so many questions. Were my experiences of seeing Grandad and the other spirit forms intended just to wake me up spiritually? Would I always be able to see spirits or would it wear off? What did it all mean? Where was it all taking me? Was I a medium? I sat for hours with these questions. Hours turned into weeks and then months. Sometimes I got a response when I asked such questions of my inner self, and sometimes I didn't. I soon realised that the more desperate I was to get an answer to something, the less likely it was I would get a response. I found that I had to ask questions in a curious way rather than a demanding way and not as though my whole life depended on the response. Some subjects I asked questions about did not get a response at all no matter how I asked. I didn't know if I was asking the wrong questions or whether I was asking them in the wrong way. Sometimes I would get the response to a question days later when I was doing something mundane, such as washing the dishes.

One thing I did come to realise is that when we ask for help, our questions need to be specific. If we just ask for help and nothing happens it is because our request is not specific enough. The universe does not know how to respond. If we ask for help with a specific aspect of a particular issue we usually get the help we have asked for. It is not always, however, the solution that we thought it might be or that we wanted. And we have to be aware of and prepared to notice all the signs.

As a result of all this soul-searching I decided I would love to be a medium if I could. I was impressed with the way Stephen Turoff healed people and hoped that maybe that would be a possibility too.

Prior to my own experiences, my one and only encounter with a medium was when one came to perform at the village hall and I went along to accompany my mother who was keen to attend. Mum had been told she had healing abilities. She had done nothing about it through her life, but she was curious. The medium was appalling. "Can anyone take a John from the spirit world?" the medium asked the whole left side of the room and of course someone there knew a John. If she had asked the right side of the room I felt pretty sure she would have found someone there who knew a John too, who had passed over! John is a very common name in England. I had been quite irritated by the whole charade. The messages she conveyed were vague; "Grandma's been worrying about you." and revolved mainly around the dearly departed wanting to give their loved ones here flowers, which I found really odd. I mean, if you're dead and talking to the living, wouldn't you have something more meaningful to convey? I felt she was a total con and that there was not a shred of real 'proof', for my analytical mind, in the whole show. The experience left me feeling very angry. I had

had nothing to do with psychics in any shape or form from that point on and considered myself a sceptic and a justified one at that.

This made the shift to how I now viewed things amazing. It also helps me to understand how people sometimes find my story hard to believe. Not only did I now recognise the existence of a spirit world because of my direct experience, but I was also ready to make the conscious decision to start exploring what was possible in terms of forming a relationship with it. Even if I wasn't a 'medium' as such, I was still interested in building a better understanding of my own experiences, my own psychic potential and the scientist in me now wanted to explore the true nature of our reality.

So where was I to begin? From the start, I really wanted to race out and buy a copy of 'Voices in my Head' by Doris Stokes, because the title described exactly how I felt. However, I was told internally not to read anything about mediumship and instead to have my own experiences and to learn from them.

Perhaps because of the formal academic nature of my personality, I decided instead to try seeking some information and understanding from the Institute for Psychic Studies in London whose address I had found in the phone book, so I made an appointment to meet with one of their top people. When I arrived for the appointment, I was told that the lady I was seeing would be delayed a little. I was asked if I was okay to wait and I was offered a cup of tea. I sipped my tea and took a few moments to take in the place. Two other people were waiting for interviews. They looked 'normal' enough. Books and journals filled bookcases and the main seating area was open-plan.

After a short while I was called upstairs. The lady's office was a smaller version of the waiting room downstairs and she must have been at least seventy years of age. White hair, tied up, framed a sweet face. Her age took me completely by surprise. She looked as though she ought to be retired. It took me a few moments to find my words.

When I regained my composure, I explained that I was having really strange experiences seeing and hearing what appeared to be dead people. I would be happy to work with a scientist to understand exactly what was happening to me and to assess its accuracy. This sweet lady with the white hair laughed, though I am sure she didn't mean to cause offence. "My dear, lots of people experience what you are experiencing," she said, somewhat dismissively I thought. She paused and then said, "You aren't anything special you know. We won't need to study you."

"But what I am seeing is really clear, really real," I protested. "I thought you would want to . . ."

She patted me on the hand. "Lots of people are like you my dear. It's nothing to worry about." and with that I was shown the door.

So now, I had been internally guided not to get help from books or the spiritualist church and yet the Institute for Psychic Studies had turned me away. Where was I to turn? I decided that if I was going to develop my abilities it would be down to me and whoever it was who was working with me. And so I resolved to work at understanding my new powers myself with the systematic approach I had taken to studies in the past. I decided to test my abilities as a medium to see if the messages I got were accurate. Accordingly, I began with my partner Manos.

We lay on the bed and I did my best to relax. I held Manos' hand, closed my eyes and I asked to see who was with him. I saw a Greek-looking lady, a man and some white steps. I felt that the lady was Manos' Grandmother. The lady held up five fingers and I somehow just knew internally that she was telling me she had five children. There had been an accident, she seemed to say, a fall on the steps. Then she showed me Manos' sister who was still alive and living in Cyprus and told me she was going to have a baby boy. I had never met Manos' sister before but my description of her was very accurate.

I opened my eyes and asked Manos what he thought. As far as Manos knew, his mum had only had three siblings, a sister and two brothers, a family of four not five. Also, he didn't know anything about his sister being pregnant. It seemed that I had got it all wrong.

Soon afterwards, however, and much to my delight, we got a call from Manos' mother to say that his sister was expecting her first child, so Manos explained about the communication we had had with his Grandmother and asked whether there had ever been a fifth child. Manos' mother confirmed that in fact there had been one more child that her mother had lost, though she did not know through what cause. Clearly I couldn't have been reading Manos' mind, because the information I gave him was not previously known by him. This confirmed that there had to be a deeper explanation than mind-reading for this phenomenon. Sure enough, as time passed, Manos' sister gave birth to a healthy baby boy. It was another validation for me that what I sensed wasn't just imagination.

Spirit communications followed for a number of friends and family members. They enabled me to practise getting my mind into the correct relaxed state to allow me to get immediate access to information. I also had to learn to do readings sitting up, rather than lying on the bed, gradually developing my relaxation technique so that I could relax at will. The information I gained was nearly always correct, but I was dreadfully slow. At times it might take me forty-five minutes or more to bring through just two or three pieces of good quality information. It was clear to me that I needed a lot more practice at developing my relaxation techniques so that the information came through readily and quickly.

As word got around, requests for mediumship trickled in from work colleagues and friends of work colleagues. Often humour came through with the messages I received, like the grandmother of one of my staff who showed me herself stuck in the snow. She had fallen and her little legs were going twenty to the dozen and making absolutely no difference to her demise. Yes, the staff member remembered the incident. It was lovely to see people's faces when they realised that their loved ones were still around and still loving them.

In the autumn I read about a training workshop being run by the National Federation of Spiritual Healers in Sunbury. I remembered that the gentleman on the tube with the white hair and the vivid blue eyes had told me I was here as a healer, so I thought this was a good chance to learn more. I didn't want to go on the workshop on my own though and so I persuaded both my mother Pat and my partner Manos to come with me. NLP was very useful at times!

Sure enough, we all attended the healing workshop and it was wonderful. The trainers, Jack and Jan Angelo, were possibly the most beautiful souls I had ever met. They created a loving and safe environment for the group to explore spiritual energies and to discover for themselves how to heal others.

I certainly wanted to learn to heal but now I also realised, that I wanted to be more like Jack and Jan, more peaceful and more loving. One of the things that they said helped them most to be calm and peaceful, was to meditate. I had never tried meditating before and so this course also became my first experience of meditation. I remembered Stephen Turoff had also recommended meditation during his message, yet I had done nothing more about it since.

Before the start of each day Jack or Jan would light a candle and we then sat silently as a group for about ten minutes or so, initially gazing at the candle and then imagining taking the light within us. I realised that I almost never took the time to just sit and do nothing. At first, it felt quite strange to do so, to just sit still and do nothing for a period of time. Feelings of guilt arose in me. I felt that I should be doing something. It took some getting used to before I could just relax and let myself go during these meditations, but eventually I did. I became aware of just how active my mind was, always thinking about things that had happened or that might happen. My mind, it seemed, was constantly running away with me, following different chains of thought and consequently creating emotions within me. Slowly, I came to enjoy sitting quietly and just being.

As part of the workshop, we learnt to sense the aura in and around the physical body. We were then taken through a structured process sensing energies from the head to the toe and allowing the energies to flow through us. As we did so, we identified pockets of high energy or blockages that indicated problem areas that needed healing.

The workshop was better than a holiday. We all left feeling inspired and refreshed. We had all learnt so much and were keen to try our new-found skills. Manos was very open-minded and enjoyed the learning and meditation. Mum did well but needed more practise before she could do healings for others, regularly. I was really keen to put what I had learnt into practice.

We were hopeful that the peace and love of the workshop was going to be carried back into our day-to-day lives. Such hopes didn't last long for me though. I returned to work to find my line manager had summoned me to Birmingham to see him.

It was a two-hour drive to Birmingham, three hours at peak times, and of course my manager wanted to see me early so it took the extra hour. I wondered if he set that time deliberately or whether he was just unaware of the consequences of such actions on others. My gut feel about the meeting was not good and my gut proved correct. I was given three orders; not to talk to anyone else about my experiences, to stop demonstrating what I could do to anyone, bank employee or otherwise and to go back to those people I had already spoken to and play down my abilities. I was given twenty-four hours to reflect on my decision.

I reflected and realised I couldn't stop talking about what I had experienced, partly because the experiences had affected me so greatly but partly also because I felt that people had the right to know that there is no death. I conveyed my decision to my line manager the next morning and I questioned his authority to give me such orders. I was advised that an appointment would now be made for me to see the personnel manager.

The appointment with the personnel manager meant another trip to Birmingham but this time at least, it was at a more reasonable hour so I could avoid the heaviest of the traffic. As you may be able to imagine, I was very nervous about the meeting. I had shifted in a matter of months from being an exemplary employee, promoted through the organisation at a young age, to refusing to obey my line manager and facing a disciplinary visit to the personnel manager. I wondered as I drove, whether I should have consulted a solicitor before attending but it was too late now. I decided honesty was the best policy.

Thankfully, the personnel manager was more tolerant and, in fact, a lot more reasonable than I had expected him to be. I was as honest as possible with him about what had happened to me and what was happening to me. I explained that in the light of my experiences I would probably be leaving the bank to develop my abilities full time and that in the meantime I felt that I needed to practise. I wasn't charging anyone for what I was doing and I didn't consider it was affecting my work other than by making my line manager uneasy. The personnel manager thought about what I said and concluded that as far as he was concerned he would not object to me offering mediumship or even charging for it so I could start to build up business prior to leaving the bank!

Imagine my line manager's response when he heard this! I expected smoke to come out of his ears! Our relationship immediately deteriorated further with him threatening to change me over with the Birmingham training manager so I could be in the same office as him and under his day-to-day supervision. Some people react strongly when presented with something that they don't understand or that doesn't fit their view of reality.

I desperately wanted to develop my psychic abilities full time, but I felt that I couldn't really afford to give up my generous salary and company car, although I didn't know how much longer I could stay working at the bank either. I knew I didn't want to spend my life like this any more; not when so much more was possible. I remember experiencing a vivid realisation of how I would feel on my deathbed if I was still a bank manager and hadn't explored what else was possible. It was after that vision that I made the internal commitment to leave the bank and to see where the spiritual path led. I asked the highest part of me to help me take the best possible path. Would it be as a spiritual medium? I just had to be patient a bit longer. It seemed like an eternity before the time was right, but it was in fact only a few months.

They say every cloud has a silver lining and as it turned out there was a positive side to my line manager's behaviour. Our deteriorating relationship made it easier for me to make the final decision to leave the bank in which I had been employed since I was a sixteen year old! In fact, it got to the point that I couldn't wait to leave the bank.

In the meantime I decided that it was now time to meet face-to-face with Alison Harper, the psychic astrologer who had given me such an accurate reading over the telephone. I was intrigued to find out what she would be like and what else she would be able to tell me. Alison had shoulder-length auburn hair. She was very well groomed and had a friendly disposition. Unlike many psychics, she had been a professional person, an art teacher, before she started developing her psychic abilities. I trusted her completely, partly because of her accuracy in the first reading she had given me over the phone and partly because she came across as a really regular, down-to-earth and open person.

Alison looked at my future psychically and saw me on a stage in front of hundreds of people. She saw that I was working for a charity of some kind and that I was wearing a vivid blue dress, like the blue on her computer screen, but she couldn't tell me what it was I was actually doing.

Alison suggested joining a psychic development circle. She said that they ran one at their office in Croyden and that I might like to give it a try sometime. I had relocated now to Tadcaster in North Yorkshire so each month I would travel all the way from Tadcaster near Leeds to Croydon in Surrey, a journey of about four hours each way. But it was worth it. I learnt about different aspects of psychic development; tarot cards, psychometry, clairvoyance, seeing my own past lives and seeing the past lives of others. There were different people there every time I went. I didn't really make friends as such as I lived so far away but there were always different people to practise on. The teachers seemed genuinely impressed with what I was able to tell them. We didn't, however, learn about mediumship or talking to spirit world. I discovered that there are a lot of psychics but not many mediums, so that side of things I had to continue to develop by myself.

One week I happened to arrive early for the development class and that was when I noticed a photograph in one of the offices. The photograph was of a man in an orange robe with an afro hair style. I immediately recognised it as the same man I had seen in the photographs at Stephen Turoff's healing centre. I asked who he was and remembered the name once told – Sai Baba. This time I wrote down the name and decided it was time to find out more about this enigmatic character.

In Search of a Teacher

I found the psychic development classes with Alison's group useful but I still wanted to further develop my mediumship and I wanted a teacher who was closer to home. Internally I asked for such a teacher and within a few weeks I thought I had at last found him.

To qualify as a spiritual healer you have to work for some time with an existing healer. It had taken some time for the NFSH to advise me of suitable healers in my area. When they did, I had the choice of two; a lady and a gentleman. Instinctively I chose the lady, but she was not in a position to work with another trainee at that time so I had to settle for the gentleman. I spoke with him on the phone. He sounded kind and supportive. I talked about wanting to develop my mediumship abilities too and he said he was a medium himself and would be delighted to assist me. I was over the moon. At last I had found a teacher.

All went well for the first visit or two and he proved himself to be helpful and knowledgeable. He talked about a pledge I needed to make to spirit world. They had never mentioned this to me on the NFSH course, but it seemed reasonable enough. He explained to me that I had to decide what I wanted to say and that we would meet to do the ceremony the next day.

I arrived the following day as planned and for the first time his wife wasn't there. He read through what I had written and talked about this being a sacred ceremony and so it was best done skyclad (another word for in the nude). I wasn't happy about that. He explained it was so that spirit could see that I was holding nothing back. I knew absolutely that what he was saying had far more to do with the physical world than the spiritual world. I began to feel worried that I knew very little about this man whose home I was now in. I assessed him and realised that he was very sturdy, that I would have little chance of escaping if he restrained me, and that his behaviour was concerning to me. I quickly checked in my mind where the exits were. To get out of the house I had to get through three doors and past a dog. If I screamed no one would hear me. The other houses were too far away. What if there were other men in the house? I decided for safety's sake to play along for a while.

I said there was no way I could possibly take off all my clothes and pretended that I had a hang-up about my body. He said he would lend me a sacred gown to wear instead. I put on what he called 'the sacred gown'. It covered me from neck to wrists and ankles. I felt I just had to get through this and then not come back. I was by this stage in fear of my life but surprisingly calm in my head.

After his hocus-pocus ceremony, he said, "Now we need to bond."

"What do you mean by that?" I asked with feigned naivety.

"What do you think I mean?" he replied.

"Hold hands?" I offered.

"That would be a good start," he said, "but we need something that will bring us even closer."

"I can only think of one thing and we aren't doing that!" I blurted.

I had him all wrong, he assured me. He was impotent and I could ask his wife if I needed verification of that fact. In all seriousness he explained that this was a sacred spiritual ceremony necessary so that as my teacher he would be able to help me whenever I needed help. There needed to be a blending of energies he told me, assuring me earnestly that it was worse for him as when he went through his ceremony he had to do it with a man. How I kept from laughing at that point I don't know, but it was probably the fear.

In the end he lay on top of me on the lounge floor. It was a compromise I played along with, as it was preferable to being raped or worse. It was awful; really uncomfortable. I felt sick to the pit of my stomach and prayed it would be over soon. Eventually, his little ceremony was over and I arranged to see him the next day. Instead I went straight to the police.

The conversation went something like this;

"Now why exactly did you go to see this man?"

"To help me develop as a medium and a healer."

"What is a medium?"

"Someone who sees and talks to dead people."

"And you do that do you?"

"Yes."

"How long have you been doing that for?"

"For a year or so."

"And what was this man's house like?"

"An ordinary house."

"There weren't any things out of the ordinary there?"

"Not unless you call crystals and red light out of the ordinary. It was just a regular house."

"And he didn't actually touch you?"

"Sort of. He lay on top of me."

"But you let him lie on top of you."

"Yes, because I feared for my life. I felt I needed to play along with him."

"And what is he like this man?"

"He seems like a really nice friendly man."

"Okay we'll look into it."

The police had no record against his name and they explained that he could have been a sexual offender but that if he changed his name and address they would have no way of knowing.

I telephoned the National Federation of Spiritual Healers. At least they should know, I thought. A younger person going along to him might not escape as lightly as I had done. I knew it would be my word against his. Over the telephone, I explained all that had happened to me and was told that they'd had no previous complaints against him. He hadn't actually technically committed an offence, so there was nothing that they could do. He would get off scot-free. I was exasperated so I wrote him a letter saying I would not be seeing him again and that in my view my spiritual progress was not determined by taking off my clothes and bonding with others in the way he had suggested. I posted the letter through his letterbox at a time I felt that his wife would be most likely to open the mail. I didn't hear from him again.

It was undoubtedly one of the worst lessons I have had in this lifetime but I took from it that first and foremost I must listen to my feelings and not give away my power to others. I felt sick to the pit of my stomach whenever I thought about the whole incident.

I was getting by at work but most of my energies were going into reading about spiritual matters and practising my new skills as a medium, clairvoyant and tarot reader. I was both relieved and excited then, when a voice one day said, "It's time to leave the bank." I had known this moment was going to arrive eventually and I felt calm about it despite the major change it would make in my life. I tendered my resignation and agreed to work two months notice to give time for my replacement to be found.

Prior to this I had been invited back to Regent's College to help assist on that year's NLP course. I was amazed to be invited after my experiences of seeing dead people the previous year, but very flattered to be asked, so I jumped at the chance of going through the training again. It had been an excellent course. The course fell during the two months notice period too, so it would only be a few weeks that I would actually have to work at the bank. I reassured myself I could get through it. Only a few weeks more!

The first month passed fairly uneventfully, except that by now I was even getting requests to work as a medium for managers and senior managers, more than one of whom swore me to secrecy. It would be very hard for them to be taken seriously and to strike the fear of God into the junior managers if the junior managers knew they consulted the likes of me. I began to see many of the managers in a different light.

The NLP course was like a breath of fresh air. Each year a number of students from the previous year's course are invited to help assist. This approach both helped the new people get maximum support and helped the assisting students reinforce the learning of the previous year's course.

I threw myself into the learning once more and the course went along fairly normally until one of the other assistants, Nic, asked if I would do some healing on his back. I had mentioned during the introductions that I had recently done a training course with the National Federation of Spiritual Healers. I forgot about his request until later that day when he reminded me. He was in a lot of pain and pleaded with me to do some healing on him before I left that night. I explained that I was only a beginner. He still wanted some healing and so I stayed behind at the end of the course.

I asked him to lie down on the floor. I closed my eyes, held my hands out over his back and relaxed. "Now we will show you how to really heal," came a voice in my head.

I told Nic what I had heard and said, "I don't know what is happening but just trust it."

"Get out of your head," said the voice.

I imagined myself going out of my body to the back of the room. My hands moved and straight away my consciousness was back in my head. Three 'guides' were present. One had my hands, one had Nic's arms and one had his legs. I didn't see them but I could sense them. I wanted to see what my hands were doing. I again imagined myself going out of my body and to the back of the room. Nic's legs started to move and I opened an eye to see what was happening; yes I was back in my head again. I wanted to know what was going on.

I said, "Show me and teach me. I am curious. I don't just want to be out of things. Let me go somewhere I can learn about this!" I imagined myself going up some stairs.

Nic moaned and his spine clicked and I was back in my body. And so it went on. I tried to get my consciousness out of my body, then my hands would move or Nic would groan and I would be back in my head. I guess the whole healing would have taken about twenty minutes.

When the healing finished, Nic and I both knew at the same time. Whoever or whatever had been with us had left. This was my first guided experience with such intensity. I had sensed three energy beings in the room assisting me. All I could say was a swear word which I won't repeat. I just said it again and again. What we had both experienced had just blown apart our sense of reality. Nic was as shocked as I was. He explained that he had a twisted pelvis, compacted vertebrae and a curvature of the spine. He was seeing a chiropractor twice a week just to stay vertical. Now his back felt absolutely fine and I hadn't laid a finger on him. What was even more amazing is that as he was lying face-down on the floor, he felt his legs being lifted up until they were at a ninety-degree angle to his body, something we both considered impossible. I was so glad I hadn't seen that. I would have totally freaked.

The next day news about the healing spread quickly. Nic had visited his chiropractor who upon examining him, confirmed his back was no longer a problem. He got just one click out of it and turned down Nic's request for an x-ray saying there was no need as his back was now fine. The chiropractor understandably wanted to know what had happened and Nic did his best to explain. I would have loved to be a fly on the wall!

I didn't have to wait long to find out whether I would be able to do it again. An older gentleman attending the course approached me during the break to ask whether I would be able to help him. I honestly didn't know but said I would try and we agreed to get together at the end of the day. The gentleman was a retired builder with a badly injured knee that he was waiting to have replaced by surgery.

At the end of the course he and I went outside and he lay face-upwards on the grass. I knelt to one side of him, closed my eyes and waited. My hands started to move. I observed them moving and didn't resist what was happening. Strong, sweeping movements pulled energy from the left hip down the leg to beyond the foot, then circles and straight lines, then big, sweeping movements again. I felt as though I was pulling his legs longer. My heart was racing. It was strenuous work moving the energies. The whole healing took about fifteen minutes.

"How does that feel?" I asked when the healing came to a close.

"Great!" he said, standing up. "Pain free!" he exclaimed as he flexed and put pressure on his injured knee.

He had not expected me to be able to do anything for him really. He explained that a ton of concrete had fallen on his knee and x-rays showed it to be in bits.

"If you could bottle whatever it was you did, you'd make a fortune!" he laughed. [1]

It was time to go home and I made my way back through the park. As I walked, my arms started moving wildly in circles and straight lines just as they had when I was healing. I had no control over them. I was so grateful that there were unusually few people in the park that evening. I had enough to deal with without having to suffer further embarrassment. I was excited now though, to have performed two healings of very different people with very different ailments. The logical conclusion I came to was that the healing was clearly not just something that happened for Nic's benefit. It now seemed to be something I could do at will.

The next day Graham, the senior assistant on the course, asked for healing to assist with a breathing problem. It was just the opportunity I needed to test out my theory. I asked Graham to lie down and held my hands a foot or so over his body. Then I relaxed. Sure enough my hands started to move, slowly at first and then more definitely. My hands moved downwards closer to his body. I felt my hands go into his chest and it was as though his skin wrapped around my wrists sealing the whole area.

Immediately I was back in my body with my eyes wide open. My physical hands were well above his body after all – but it had felt so real. I closed my eyes again and the healing restarted where it had left off. This time I ignored the sensations of hands going into flesh and kept my eyes closed until all movement had stopped and I was given a sign that the healing was complete. Graham reported that his breathing had improved.

I realised at a deep level that the healing ability I was now experiencing was the direct result of my decision to trust. I had given up my career with no idea of what I was going to do. I had made a leap of faith. Inside I had made a commitment to research the spiritual side of life to the best of my abilities and in doing so, I had effectively put my faith in the universe. The universe had reciprocated by showing me just what was possible. For the first time in my life I felt truly alive and that life really was worthwhile. I at last knew that there is a reason why we are here; that it isn't all just chance. I was so happy, so inspired and so at peace all at the same time. As I went to bed that night I asked to see who my helpers were and just before falling asleep I saw three pairs of eyes, one after the other.

The day after Nic's remarkable healing he wanted to talk to me about something that was concerning him. From time to time since the healing he had experienced a force pushing his head back and then opening his mouth. What did it mean? Should he stop it or allow it? I didn't have a clue. I didn't really understand what he meant until later that afternoon. At the end of each day we would often finish with a visualisation of some kind to help integrate the learning. The weather was so good the trainer decided to take us all outside. The assistants were invited to join the participants for this particular exercise. We all lay on the grass and closed our eyes and the trainer gently guided us through the visualisation.

My usually good concentration was disturbed by my hands starting to move. They came up from my sides and locked together at the front of my waist. Then they started to jerk up and down in small movements. It was totally out of my control, or so it felt. My locked hands were gently moving up my body and up to my head. I felt perfectly safe and trusted the process. I was concerned about how it must look, but I didn't feel I should stop the process. My hands continued to move up over my head and I felt myself touching another person. He started to jerk, gently at first. I came back to normal and opened my eyes to see that the person lying next to me was Nic. His jerking got stronger and stronger. The guided visualisation was coming to an end and I was starting to worry what would happen when everyone saw Nic. I knew Nic was safe and that it was important not to disturb the process.

The jerking intensified and by the time people had sat up it looked like either an epileptic fit or a huge orgasm wracking his body. People were starting to get concerned. I said, "It's alright, don't touch him. He will be right in a moment." The shaking stopped abruptly and Nic confirmed he was absolutely fine. I wasn't fine, however. I felt that people were looking at me as though I was a witch. What was happening had disrupted the course and I didn't feel comfortable returning there the next day. I spoke with Graham the senior assistant and he agreed it would be a good idea for me to keep my head down for a day or two. As I reflected on the afternoon's events I realised how everything connected together. Usually I felt my hands being taken over as I was doing a healing. Today someone had taken over my hands when I was just relaxing. I had the answer to Nic's questions; the pushing back of his head and the 'fit' were the final parts of his healing, clearing an energy block in his spine.

One of the other assistants who had seen the whole thing said he knew of a lady who had studied Native American spirituality and he suggested that perhaps she could help. We went to see her that evening and I poured out all that had happened. She suggested using automatic handwriting to communicate with whoever was with me. For automatic handwriting you relax your whole body, particularly the arm and hand you write with and then you ask a question. If spirit could move my hands to heal they could surely move my hands to write. There was a lot of scribbling to start with and then it settled down.

"Who are you I asked?"

"Grandad," came the reply.

"What do you want?"

"You are in great danger . . . people are after you . . . they want what you have." I started to get anxious.

"You must go way from here," it continued. "You must go somewhere safe." My anxiety increased.

"This doesn't feel right," the spiritual lady said. "Check it is your granddad."

"How?" I asked.

"Ask who it is, three times," she replied. "There is a natural law that they have to answer truthfully if asked three times."

It sounded odd to me but I did as instructed. "Who are you?"

"Grandad," the writing spelled.

"Who are you?" I asked again.

"Grandad," came the reply once more.

"Who are you?" I asked for the third time.

"Hee, Hee, Hee . . ." I had a spirit with me that was playing games trying to create fear within me so that it could better attach itself to me or to enable other spirits to attach.

The spiritual lady helped me to banish the spirit. Today I am not so sure that it was the right thing to do. The spirits I have had dealings with since have never been evil though they have occasionally been misguided. Usually when you talk to them about what they want it is not usually to do us harm but to get something they want. If you help them get what it is they want, they usually leave without a fuss.

Back then, however, I had only very limited experience and I was feeling afraid. I wondered how I could protect myself against such interference. The spiritual lady was going to see a visiting Buddhist Lama in London the following day. She asked if I would like to accompany her and receive a blessing. She said that if there were anything in my space that shouldn't be there a blessing would certainly take care of it. It was perfect timing. I think the only things I knew about Buddhism at that time were that Buddhists shaved their heads and that Richard Gere was a supporter.

The visiting Buddhist Lama's name was Penor Rinpoche, the head of Buddhist teaching. I think it was his first visit to the United Kingdom. The spiritual lady and I were the first to arrive at the venue, as she was determined that we should arrive early to get a good seat. We chatted on the steps outside as we waited and I came to realise that Buddhists come from all walks of life and that they don't necessarily shave their heads. I still didn't know what to expect. Eventually the doors were opened and we got a good seat near the front. I quickly made friends with an American girl sitting next to me. She wanted to know if I had been into Buddhism for a long time. I told her a bit about what had been happening to me and that I knew nothing about Buddhism. She explained that today was an empowerment; a high empowerment. Her feeling was that I must be very special for events to have conspired to get me there on that one day.

The prayers started in what I presumed must be Tibetan and I started to get really sleepy. I mean really sleepy. I could hardly keep my eyes open. I didn't want to appear rude or disrespectful and I couldn't understand why I was so tired. I had slept well the previous night. I wondered whether perhaps it was all the stress of the past few days. My body started moving slowly backwards and forwards in a rhythm with the chanting. I was so tired; it was very hard to keep my eyes open. I tried every trick I knew. Forcing my fingernails into my thighs, clenching and unclenching my toes. I have never been so tired in my life. My eyelids were like lead. I was determined not to fall asleep. It would be so rude.

A golden light popped on in the front of the right-hand side of my head. I checked I hadn't just fallen asleep. I checked I wasn't imagining it. No! There it was, a little golden light in my head moving very slowly. It took a few moments to move across and then disappeared as suddenly as it had appeared. The experience raised my energy for a little while and then I was back trying desperately not to fall asleep. I was so glad when there was finally an interval. "How are you?" The American girl asked. I told her what I had experienced and how I was so sleepy throughout it. "How do you feel now?" she asked. I felt fine, not sleepy at all. "In the second half," she suggested, "watch the monks and what they do."

I did as she suggested and noted that the monks were in as sleepy a state as I was, rocking forward and back with the same rhythm as I had felt. I felt so much better that I relaxed. I wasn't tired after all; it was a phenomenon of the empowerment. I enjoyed the second half, although I didn't understand much of what was said and I didn't fall asleep but was just pleasantly drowsy throughout.

By the next day, I was feeling much better and returned to assist on the course. I wasn't spoken to directly about the incident but the trainer made an announcement to all concerned that the course was about NLP and that this was what we all needed to concentrate on. I was happy with that, so with no further requests for healing, the course finished without further incident and I returned home with just two weeks of my notice to work.

I didn't know what I would be doing once those two weeks expired, but I felt that the healing experiences had validated my decision to resign. Pieces of the jigsaw were starting to come together. I was feeling that there was some higher power looking after me and making sure that I was always in the right place at the right time.

I was curious about what my new career would be now that I only had ten working days left as a bank manager!

A New Career

One morning a few days before my leaving date an advert in the local newspaper jumped out at me. The headline shouted, 'Psychic Fair'. Top mediums and clairvoyants were visiting York, twenty minutes or so from where I lived. The advert also said that they wanted more 'readers'. I couldn't believe it. Maybe this was my new career pathway. Surely this was a huge opportunity to practise my skills on a wide variety of people as well as to meet and work with other psychics. I rang the number excitedly and spoke with a man named John. John invited me to go along to meet him and talk about what would be involved in joining the professional psychic group that toured the UK.

I had never been to a psychic fair and I didn't know quite what to expect and after my scare from the 'medium' teacher I didn't want to go alone, so I took my partner Manos with me. Manos was equally curious about what a psychic fair was and what I would be letting myself in for. The psychic fair was held at a hotel in York. There was a small admission fee and as we entered we were directed to sit with forty or so other people who formed an audience of sorts. We were told that John, the organiser, would be explaining all about the fair.

It took me a few moments to take in the scene. There was subdued lighting and candles burned on many of the tables at the far side of the room giving a soft glow to the people who were sitting there. Voices were kept hushed so you couldn't entirely make out what was being said. Just the occasional word was audible. There was a strange yet familiar smell in the room. Manos thought it must be incense burning. The music that was playing was relaxing and helped put me at ease. I liked it.

I glanced around the rows of chairs near where I was seated. Most of the audience was women with just a handful of men present. The average age would have been about fifty years old but there were also a fair number of young girls. I had never previously been remotely interested in attending a psychic fair so I was quite surprised at how popular it seemed to be. The people attending looked like regular people from all walks of life.

John came in, introduced himself and explained that the six people sitting at the back of the room were called 'readers'. Each reader had different abilities. Some were able to read palms (palmistry), some could read handwriting (graphology), all could read tarot cards, some were psychic and two could talk to the deceased. Each reader had a timetable list on his or her table. If we would like to have a reading with someone, all we had to do, he said, was to put our names on their list and they would call us over when they were ready to see us. Prices for readings varied from fifteen pounds to twenty-five pounds, which I thought was very expensive considering that you didn't know if someone was genuine or not. John explained to the audience that we really needed to trust our own intuition to determine who we went to.

"Just trust your feelings," he said. That was easier said than done.

Five of the readers were female and one was male. Readers had a tablecloth on the table in front of them and each reader had a different theme. A couple of the readers looked like gypsies. Most had candles, crystals and other ornaments on their tables. They had signs advertising what they did and some even had leaflets. I pondered who I would be most drawn to and why. Who would attract me?

The busiest lady by far was a lady called Vanessa. Her table was decorated in pale pink and magenta, which made a refreshing change from all the others which were mainly dark coloured – blacks, silver and gold. Vanessa's waiting list was already twice the size of anyone else's and yet she charged more. I was intrigued. I wondered whether the audience knew her from past visits or whether it was just the impression she gave that made her so popular. The client sitting with Vanessa started to cry, which caused a flurry of names to be added to Vanessa's list. Manos and I were now both keen to see what Vanessa could do, but I decided we were better to spread ourselves around so I chose to try someone else and left him to visit Vanessa.

I opted for a woman who looked like a gypsy. What a waste of money! The 'gypsy' reader was so far off the mark it was laughable. She told me more about her alcoholic partner and the problems in her life than she did about me. I didn't tell her how far out she was, but paid her fee of twenty pounds and went back to my seat. Manos' reading with Vanessa was very accurate. He was very impressed and so was I when he relayed what he had been told.

I waited for things to quieten down a bit before introducing myself to John. John talked me through what I would need to join the psychic fair; a cloth, cards, signs, leaflets and how much I would need to pay him. He asked how soon I could start. We agreed on a date and that was it. There was no test of my abilities. I had expected to have to do a reading for him at the least, but he took me at my word.

Perhaps he could tell just from talking to me that I was genuine.

The group was one of two touring parties of professional clairvoyants and mediums[2] that travelled through the UK. By professional, I mean that they did their spiritual work full-time, not necessarily that they were of a professional standard. Although obviously the regular ones were.

The ease with which I had joined the psychic group completely surprised me and concerned me a little. But I wanted to put my emerging skills into practice and I decided that working from 2pm to 11pm four days a week at a psychic fair would be a good ground breaking experience. Having now sampled a whole raft of new-age practices from healing workshops to Buddhism, I felt that working at the fair would also give me more of an idea of where I fitted into the scheme of things. I had just two weeks to get together everything I needed.

In the meantime I received a phone call from Nic, the gentleman whose back I had worked on at the NLP course. His back was still great and he claimed that I had already saved him a small fortune in chiropractor's bills. Nic had a favour to ask. He wondered how I would feel about seeing a colleague of his, an MP at the House of Commons who had a sore shoulder. I agreed but immediately started to worry about what I was letting myself in for. I had never been to the House of Commons before. What if the healing didn't work? What if I made Nic look foolish? What if I made myself look foolish? What if my hands didn't move and nothing happened?

Fortunately I didn't have too long to stress myself out. The appointment was made for a few days time, as there was some urgency. It was a four hour drive down to London so I made arrangements to stay with a friend. Nic met me and we travelled to the House of Commons together. I was very nervous and was glad that Nic had taken care of everything. We had to collect security passes at the main gate and I worried about what I would say if someone asked me the purpose of my visit. Thankfully no one did and we were able to meet with the MP at the appointed time.

The MP's room was like nothing I had ever seen before. The decor was old and worn, but looked as though it would originally have been top quality. A computer was incongruously placed on top of the main desk. It looked totally out of place with the rest of the furniture, which dated from a different century.

Nic introduced me to the MP as the lady he had spoken of previously who may be able to help with his shoulder. The MP had already had an operation on his shoulder but still could not move it fully. I explained that I didn't really understand what happened when I healed, only that it worked and that while healing I wouldn't need to touch him, but just to work in the space around his body. The MP seemed happy enough with this explanation and moved into a different chair so I could get all the way around him. He seemed a very pleasant gentleman.

I closed my eyes and did my best to relax. I focused on my breathing and tried to 'forget' about my hands. Thankfully my hands started moving almost straight away. Forwards, backwards, small circles, bigger circles – away from the body and towards the body they went, forcefully at first and then very gently and then forcefully again. At no time did I touch the MP's body and I think this took him something by surprise even though I'd told him that this was how I would work. The healing lasted between fifteen and twenty minutes and then I was given a sign it was complete. The MP seemed surprised; after all I didn't appear as though I had done anything. I asked the MP to try moving the affected limb. It moved with ease, the pain had gone and he had full mobility once more. He was delighted!

Though I had now done successful healing sessions for some time, I was getting ready to join the psychic fair, so my attention became firmly focused on my psychic abilities. My first psychic fair was to be in the south of England and I would need to stay away from home for four nights a week. My mother Pat needed some time out from her relationship and was fascinated by what was happening to me. So we decided to travel and stay together. This would mean I would have some support and that she would have a much-needed break.

Learning to work at the psychic fair was a steep learning curve. Previously, I had only worked alone. Working with other people around me took some getting used to. I wasn't sure how I was going to handle it. Everyone seemed to work so differently to me. On my first day, I had an unexpected setback. My first client refused to pay. The lady complained that I hadn't told her anything she did not already know. I was surprised. I know when the information I am given is correct because the hairs on my arms stand on end.

"Was there any part of the reading you felt wasn't right?" I enquired.

"No," she said, "but it was just the same information as I got in a reading I had done by another psychic." I remembered my earlier bank training – the customer is always right – and gave her money back. I also remembered the reading I had been given at the psychic fair in York, which had not been accurate. What if I wasn't good enough at this?

A wave of panic engulfed me. I had walked out of a perfectly good, well-paid job into an unknown area without first checking that I was good enough to do this professionally. What had I been thinking? I should have practised more first and built up more gradually. How could I charge fifteen pounds if I wasn't good enough? What if all my clients wanted their money back? Mum did her best to reassure me that I was good enough and to stick at it.

The day was quiet in terms of customers attending the fair and I had to wait about an hour before I got another client. My stomach churned. I tried not to think too much about that first client. I was pleased to find that my next client was very different. This lady was genuinely pleased with the reading, and so were my subsequent clients. My confidence started to grow and the panic eased. The more my confidence grew, the quicker the information came through. All I had to do was relax. I earned enough to pay for my table and the night's accommodation for Mum and me. After a shaky start, my first day had actually gone very well, but I was still questioning whether I had done the right thing. After all why would anyone in their right mind choose to be a psychic reader and risk complete ridicule when they could continue to be a successful bank manager? Later that evening I reflected on the day's events. My new career, if you could call it that, had begun. I was glad that I had heeded Mum's advice to stick with it.

But working in my new career as a psychic wasn't as glamorous as it may have at first appeared and I earned only a fraction of what I was earning at the bank. It can appear that readers are earning a lot of money but after paying for your table, your share of advertising and room hire, you also have to pay for your accommodation, fuel and meals. Unless the fairs are busy you don't make that much, certainly nowhere near as much as I was used to earning.

The hours were intense. Mediumship is tiring if you are really busy but funnily enough, even more so if you are really quiet. At night it would sometimes be difficult to get to sleep, especially if you forgot to close down psychically. Add to that a few fairs with small audiences and you can struggle to keep going. It does tend to weed out the not so good ones though, which I suppose is a good thing. As the youngest and newest addition to the group, I always seemed to be the last one to get a client, especially if only a few people came.

Vanessa, the most experienced psychic, seemed always to be the first to get a client and would work steadily, along with one or two of the others. The rest of us would just sit there. Vanessa had worked on the psychic fairs for some years and appeared very confident. I was fascinated to see how she worked and how quickly she was able to bring through information for clients, switching between mediumship and clairvoyance at will. I wished I could work as quickly and I decided to learn as much as I could from her. At first it was difficult to get to know Vanessa but later we became good friends.

After a while, I started reading a book during the quiet times. John caught me. "No, no, no!" he said. "You will never get clients that way." John suggested that in the quiet times I might gaze into a crystal ball I had bought for display on my table. I explained I couldn't see anything in the crystal ball. I had tried but it just didn't work for me. "Not a worry," he said. "It'll look good!" It must have looked good, or perhaps it caused me to relax because I started to attract more clients and there was much less down time. It also meant I was starting to do better than break-even.

My skills as a medium and a clairvoyant were steadily increasing and I couldn't help but notice at the fairs how certain kinds of people would be attracted to me, while other readers would attract other types of people towards them. I attracted more spiritual people; people who wanted answers and who wanted to find out why they were here. They were mirrors for my own internal searching. As I helped them find their answers I also found answers for myself, and a lot more questions! My information also started to come through much more quickly.

I remember doing a clairvoyant reading for one young man at a town not far from Glastonbury. I was shown clairvoyantly how all the experiences of past lifetimes had brought this young man to this particular point in time, in this particular physical body to demonstrate all that he had learned. His work on the earth was to specialise in vibration. I wasn't shown specifically what he did in past lifetimes. I didn't need to know. I knew though that he understood exactly what I meant. I could see it in his face. He went back to join his partner sitting in the audience, thrilled that I had confirmed for him what he knew deep within. Someone had understood and reassured him that he wasn't going mad. I knew how that felt and I was so happy to be able to give him that reassurance.

At such times, giving up my career as a bank manager seemed to be so worthwhile. This is how it often is with a good reading, it resonates with us. It touches part of our soul. It might not make sense to our logical brains, we might not see how we will get there, but it feels 'right' within us. I had seen past life times before, but for the first time had a deeper insight into how they affect and influence our current lifetime.

I had become confident doing individual readings with others around but not confident about giving a reading in front of an audience. As part of the psychic fair the readers would sometimes be asked by John to do a talk to the audience about what they did and to give a small demonstration. I got away without doing one for quite a while because I was the newest member, but eventually it was my next logical step. With John's guidance I decided to do psychometry, as that is probably the easiest way to work if you are feeling nervous.

Psychometry is where you take an article belonging to someone, preferably a piece of jewellery and hold it to sense its vibration. You may then pick up clairsentient information (feelings), clairaudient information (words, sounds or music), or clairvoyant images. My strongest ability tended to be clairsentience or picking up feelings. I found that I could then develop these into images and words by saying internally, "Show me." and, "Tell me." If I needed it to be more specific I would say, "be more specific." If I didn't understand what was being conveyed, I would say, "Show me another way." or, "Tell me another way." The secret was not to try too hard. Some people are easier to read for than others. That aspect, you have little control over. Some days you are more on form than others. That aspect, you do have some control over.

My first reading to an audience went far better than I expected. I was only intending to use clairvoyance but found I had a grandmother in my head for one of the young ladies in the audience. The grandmother in spirit wanted her granddaughter to know she was all right and to remind her about the frying pan. Grandmother was laughing in my head as she said this. I asked the granddaughter what the grandmother meant and she explained that on her wedding day her grandmother had given her a frying pan and joked about using it on her husband if he didn't do as he was told. The whole audience laughed and I was able to relax and pass on more messages.

After that performance the list on my table grew. Now I knew how to stay busy at the psychic fairs, but the thought of doing readings in front of an audience was still nerve-wracking even though it had gone so well. It took some time but I started to enjoy the psychic fairs. I had become friends with the other readers and was particularly drawn towards Vanessa.

Vanessa was about ten years older than me and she had a wicked sense of humour. Her humour masked a more serious, sensitive side to her nature. Vanessa had been able to see spirit forms from a young age. Where my childhood had been idyllic, Vanessa's had been traumatic. At the fairs she often attracted clients who had been emotionally or sexually abused in childhood. Vanessa had a theory that mediums were either abused as children or experienced a near death experience early in life. All the mediums she had met and there had been many, fitted either category. It seemed a strange theory but yes, I had to admit that I had nearly drowned at a young age. It was one of the pieces of information Stephen Turoff gave me when I met him and I considered it was significant. Vanessa could not understand why on earth I would choose to give up being a bank manager to work on the psychic fairs. In her eyes, I had so many more opportunities available to me.

Although I was beginning to enjoy the work, the travelling required was slowly taking its toll. So I decided to join a local psychic group and just travel within Yorkshire. As well as reducing the travelling it would allow me to do some private readings from home and perhaps start my healing centre. Increasingly, I was being pulled to set up my own centre. I had thought about it more and more after the healing workshop and was encouraged by my success in healing Nic and the MP. Mum was keen to be involved too. Her confidence had grown since the workshop and she had recently been doing some healing at the fairs. To the sceptics among you this may seem far-fetched, but I truly believe that we all have these abilities if we wish to use them.

Vanessa was looking for someone to help her organise some mediumship shows. She was the best medium I had seen by far and I jumped at the chance to help. Little did I know then that one day I too would be demonstrating in front of large audiences.

The opportunity arose to join a local group and I gave my notice to leave John's group. My last fair with John's group was at a place called the Miami Hotel in Chelmsford. As we pulled up to the Miami Hotel it looked vaguely familiar but I did not think I had been to Chelmsford before. Suddenly the penny dropped. It was Stephen Turoff's place. The psychic fair room adjoined his healing centre. I couldn't believe it. I quickly told Vanessa about my experience with him. Vanessa had a long-standing skin complaint and she wondered if Stephen Turoff would be able to assist her. I thought he would but the question was whether or not we would be able to get an appointment at such short notice. We decided that it was worth calling in to see and were both amazed to find Vanessa could be seen that day. Vanessa asked if I would mind accompanying her. I was happy to accompany her, as it would give me the chance to objectively observe Stephen Turoff and the spirit-being that worked with him. On entering the room it was obvious that Stephen was in the same altered state as I had witnessed before. He spent about ten minutes working on Vanessa and then turned to me in trance and said, "God has never left you." I felt as though he looked right into me and at a deep level I knew exactly what he meant. Vanessa got much relief from the healing.

Chelmsford was a quiet psychic fair but I was busy most of the time. My final clients were ones I will remember all my life. Two ladies came in and sat in front of me. The younger of the two had a young girl in spirit with her. The spirit girl had long, dark-brown hair and was dressed entirely in denim. I could see the young girl as plain as day, but she refused to talk to me. Instead she just nodded and shook her head for "Yes" and "No". I explained what I was seeing and the lady on my right, the younger one, started crying. It was her niece who had recently died. The last time she saw her alive her niece was in a funny mood and would only nod or shake her head. In the aunt's eyes my description of her niece was excellent proof.

I spent over two hours with the spirit girl's aunt and mother answering their questions as best I could. As the evening wore on all the other readers left one by one leaving me behind with these two ladies. Eventually it came time that I had to leave too, but they both were still so upset, especially the Mum, the older lady. I didn't understand why they should still be so upset. "Why are you still so upset?" I asked. "Haven't I given you all the proof you need?" The mother looked me straight in the eye and said, "You've made it worse. You can see her and I can't!" and she started crying again. I suddenly realised that I had no real compassion. I had not lost anyone like they had and I just didn't know how it felt.

For a long time after that I didn't do mediumship for anyone. Instead, I concentrated on my clairvoyance at the local psychic fairs and organising shows for Vanessa. It was with mixed feelings I went to my first psychic fair with the Yorkshire group. What a different group of people the local psychics were! For a start, many didn't charge as much for their readings as I was now charging. My charge brought a negative response from the start. With John's group the competition had always been between our group and the other touring group. With the local group the competition was between each reader in the room. I was an easy target. I was new to the group, was immediately the busiest reader and I charged more.

At the professional national psychic fair I had learned from the best how to attract people to my table. Some of the members of the local group couldn't understand why so many people were coming to my table, so they told the organiser that I was placing private adverts in papers. When I was confronted about it I was taken by surprise. I hadn't placed any adverts but even if I had I could not see why that would be a problem. I asked them to produce copies of the adverts they claimed I had placed. No adverts could be produced to support their claims and I continued to be the busiest clairvoyant in an uneasy climate.

A few weeks later a new accusation was raised. It was suggested that I was using witchcraft to draw in clients. How ridiculous! I had always steered well clear of anything remotely linked with witchcraft. I suggested that perhaps the difference was that I did have a well-written leaflet and I was recording my readings onto a cassette tape so customers would have a permanent record. Perhaps this was why I was so busy. Any of them could do the same. Despite my suggestions they insisted that I must be using witchcraft to attract my customers. The accusations against me persisted and I found that it could be very difficult to prove you are not doing something. Eventually the organiser took my word for it. I think it helped that I was an ex-bank manager.

At times I really did wonder about the weirder side of psychic fairs and the standard of some of the readers at the local fair worried me. In my time working with the fairs, I came across some very weird people who at times held even weirder beliefs. I was reassured by clairvoyant astrologer Alison Harper's words to me that I would meet some really strange people and would have to learn how to separate the 'wheat from the chaff'.

One reader I sat next to charged twenty pounds a reading and every reading would go like this; (spreading out all the cards) "My dear you really have it all happening right now, relationship, work, finances. Where would you like me to start?". (Response) "Do you know I thought you were going to say that and I can see that this has been going on for some time now and you are not really knowing what to do for the best. It's probably going to get worse before it gets better." And so it went on. I was appalled.

I was worrying about these things on the way home one night and as I put my key in the car door a voice in my head said, "Which is worse? To be such an appallingly bad reader that people make their own decisions, or to be so good they keep coming back time and time again!" I realised I'd been judgemental and I didn't judge any more after that. I made sure to educate my clients to also look for their own answers so they weren't as dependent on me. Clairvoyance gives people extra information about a situation, which should enable them to make a better quality decision. They shouldn't use it to make their decisions for them.

New Year's Day found me in tears. This was totally out of the blue. I was sitting on the sofa alone and sobs were just racking my whole body. I had not been thinking about anything in particular so where was all this emotion coming from? I suddenly realised that I had not done any healing since working on the Member of Parliament. I thought about it, and realised that I was actually afraid of demonstrating what I could really do in the healing area. I did want to be able to heal. That was more important to me than doing readings, but I didn't want to be treated as someone special. People often put you on a pedestal when you help or heal them. Whilst I had special abilities, I didn't want to be treated differently. I did want to open a healing centre, but how could I achieve this and be myself, support myself and pay the rent?

Another consideration that was also becoming significant, was how my changing lifestyle would fit in with what Manos wanted. Our aims were becoming increasingly different. I was reminded that when I had first met Manos six years previously and long before I became aware of my psychic powers, I was travelling with a girlfriend in a taxi when a man's voice in my head had said, "Manos is only here to look after you for a few years." I was not used to hearing voices and relayed what I had heard to my friend. She hadn't heard the man's voice so at the time I thought it must have been within my head. We both thought it was odd. I didn't know whose voice it was I heard but I also knew that what I was told felt true. I never heard any more 'voices' after that until my spiritual awakening at Regent's College four years later.

We had been together for several years and now with our lives taking different paths, it was time to move on. We ended our relationship very amicably and remain good friends. Manos had taught me how to feel safe again in a relationship and reminded me how to love. He had also provided a safe relationship in which I could talk about my experiences without fear of ridicule or judgement. I would miss him. He was my best friend and a truly good person but our relationship had run its natural course.

From a pragmatic viewpoint, the end of the relationship meant that Manos would be moving out of the five-bedroom house we shared and I would be paying the rent and bills alone for the first time. The place was far too big for me alone and I made arrangements to leave but it would be several months before the rental agreement expired. In the meantime I had to cover all the bills.

I was proving as popular at the local fairs as Vanessa had been at the national ones. The customers loved me but I still wasn't popular with the other readers. They believed that I was taking business away from them, taking the food out of their mouths as they termed it. One of the readers asked me for a reading and I knew I was being tested. I was nervous but managed to bring through her father-in-law who had recently passed over, giving his name and the exact circumstances of his passing. Her mouth nearly hit the table. Whatever they criticised me for after that, it couldn't be for a lack of psychic ability.

I put more time and energy into managing the shows for Vanessa but found that financially for me they were just not viable. The organisation took so much of my time for little reward and my regular household bills were starting to stack up. I had also used a lot of my savings to finance the shows. Instead I arranged to do more work at psychic fairs. But working at psychic fairs wasn't how I wanted to live my life. I knew I wanted a healing centre.

After a matter of weeks I was told that there was not a place for me at one fair and then another and another. Before very long I was doing half the fairs I had been and my income dropped accordingly. I couldn't afford to pay my rent. I still had some savings from my time at the bank but didn't want to erode them any further.

I wanted to pay my way and so I decided to organise some extra fairs myself in a different area to the one the local organiser worked in. Word soon got around to the others and it was just the excuse they needed to get rid of me completely. They were sure I was trying to take over the organiser's business. In truth, I was just trying to make a living. I didn't want to organise fairs, I wanted to do readings at them. If they had given me more opportunities to work I wouldn't have needed to organise fairs myself. My reasons fell on deaf ears. I was out, but happily so. The only thing I had learned with the local fair was how to protect myself psychically which was a useful enough lesson. If I could work in that environment I could probably work anywhere.

Internally I had wanted a change, the universe was simply reflecting that back to me. I took events as a sign that I was ready to move on to something else. What did I really want to do? I wanted to open a healing centre and that was why I had left the professional touring group in the first place. Perhaps I thought I should put more energy into this now and make it a reality.

Travelling by car a couple of days later a voice inside my head said to me, "You will have your healing centre. It will be in a town set on water and will be set on major ley lines. You will have it in two to three weeks." I wrote it down. Since I'd bought that first notebook, recording important events was still an integral part of my life. Ley lines? I had heard the term before to do with Glastonbury. I knew they were some kind of energy lines that ran around the earth. It made me wonder if I was being shown ley lines when I saw the grid of light lines around the earth just after Grandad had first communicated with me. I gave it no more thought until later that week.

I was now organising my own psychic fairs as the main source of my income. My mum wanted to continue to give spiritual healings and I had also recruited a couple of psychic readers who were very talented but lacked experience. We were a small team but worked well together. I had booked a room in a pub in a Derbyshire town. I was the first of the readers to arrive. I parked in the car park at the back of the pub and went in. It was dreadful; really, really bad. Chips had been walked into a grimy carpet, black tattered curtains drooped at the window, the place stank of stale alcohol and it had a really bad feel energetically. I was not prepared to open myself up psychically in that place and was not prepared to ask any of the other readers to do so either. I waited to see the owner, an aggressive looking woman, who was not at all pleased that we were cancelling the event at such short notice.

After cancelling the booking, I couldn't get out of the place fast enough. In my haste I fell over, grazing both wrists and knees. A voice in my head said, "Run don't walk!" The other readers were arriving and I shared with them that the fair was to be cancelled.

"Could we work anywhere else?" one of them asked. It would have to be somewhere we could put up a sign to show where we had moved to, so only the hotel on the corner would be appropriate. I asked my mum to go over to enquire. The managers said that we could set our fair up but there was no car park to unload from. Then we realised Mum had gone to the wrong building, not the one on the corner. As it wasn't visible from the first venue it would not be suitable. I was really feeling that I should not be doing this particular psychic fair. I felt sick in the pit of my stomach and knew I needed to heed the feeling.

"We are not far from Matlock," said the youngest reader. "Why don't we take the day off and go there for a picnic?" It seemed like an excellent idea, as it was a lovely summer's day. Everyone was in agreement and so off we went. As I drove out of the car park I saw a blackboard advertising that evening's band; Run Don't Walk. Surely this was no coincidence. I felt sure I had made the right decision and was on the right path once more. I also noticed that the sickly feeling in the pit of my stomach had disappeared.

I hadn't been to Matlock, a small town in the Derbyshire Dales for many years, not since I was a child. I had forgotten how beautiful it was. We found a little cafe in a quaint little courtyard and settled down to enjoy our coffee. "Wouldn't this be ideal for a healing centre," said Barbara, one of the readers. I leaned back in my chair enjoying the sunshine, and saw a 'TO LEASE' sign on the shop directly in front of us. I just had to go in.

"Is there any chance of speaking to the owner?" I politely enquired.

"Yes, I am the owner," the lady replied.

I explained that we wanted to set up a healing centre.

"This would be ideal for you," the owner said. "It is set on major ley lines." I knew I was indeed on the right path, in the right place, at the right time. Sometimes the universe makes it almost too easy for me, but I am not complaining!

"How soon are you planning to be out?" I hardly dared ask.

"Two to three weeks," came the response.

We had found our healing centre. It was exactly as it had been described; in a town set on water and set on major ley lines. The deal was signed and sure enough it was ours within the promised three weeks. Mum decided to come in as a partner and Barbara helped us to set up. We all agreed on the name of the centre; 'Inner Peace'.

Inner Peace

Inner Peace was a place where people could come to find their inner peace, inner quiet or their inner piece meaning their eternal part within. It was intended as an oasis of healing, peace and guidance.

The pretty stone building in which we had chosen to house ourselves was ideally placed in a town big enough to provide a reasonable client base. It was set in a quaint stone courtyard and, while close enough to the main road to ensure passing trade, it was far enough away to ensure it provided a peaceful haven. There was a small fountain in the courtyard, which added to the ambience and charm. A woodcarving shop was to the right of our new shop and a cafe to the left.

Matlock was a popular tourist destination for people from several of the surrounding towns. Sheffield, Nottingham and Derby were all less than an hour's drive away. There would be year-round trade. Day trips by coach from the surrounding cities to

Matlock, were very popular. Visitor numbers peaked in the summer months but winter illuminations also brought off-season tourists to the town and its neighbour, Matlock Bath.

Our main purpose in setting up the healing centre was to give Mum and me the opportunity to practise our newly discovered healing skills. We planned to offer spiritual healing initially and then to add on additional services as we became more established. We needed to put in an additional soundproof wall and door to create a healing room and the rest of the building would then be able to operate as reception for the healing centre and gift shop.

One of the most memorable moments in the setting-up process was having the internal wall installed. The shop landlord suggested the name of a local builder to put in the special soundproof wall and door we needed. We knew we had got the atmosphere right when the builder started hammering slowly in time with the New Age music we were playing and nearly fell asleep. He had never felt so relaxed and decided to buy the tape we were playing at the time. He was one of our first customers. It was a good sign.

Everything we sold in the shop had the aim of helping people to find their inner peace; relaxing music, fragrant oils and candles, self-help and spiritual books and crystals.

When we took over the lease, the interior of the shop was painted entirely in black. That was something we really had to change and it took many more coats of paint to cover than we could ever have imagined. With each new coat of paint we would think we had conquered the black and each time we would need to do another coat. Eventually it was a very soft peach colour. After we had finished painting, the shelves had to go up and the carpets had to be cleaned. Stock had to be purchased. It was amazing how much time it all took and how much money it all cost. We were very grateful it was a small building.

All in all it was a couple of weeks before we could open the doors to our first clients. Before opening, we asked the universe to bless the place and imagined filling it with love and light and healing energies. If anyone had suggested doing something like that in my bank manager days, I would not have been able to keep a straight face. It would be too bizarre! How I had changed!

From the start we had a wonderful reception from the people of Matlock. People would come in on a regular basis saying things like, "I don't know why I am here. I just had to come in." or, "I just put money in the parking meter and felt I had to come here. Why?" It was not uncommon for people to burst into tears as they came in.

They would stay and, while we listened, talk about what was happening in their lives or how they were feeling. They would leave feeling better and invariably return. We had a few regulars who made a beeline for the shop at lunchtime to 'recharge' before returning back to their stressful jobs. We even had a policeman comment on how wonderful the shop felt. He claimed he had never felt anything like it.

Fortunately we only had the one phone call to enquire if we did 'relief massage'. Luckily I didn't take the phone call, as if I had I'm sure I wouldn't have understood what the gentleman caller meant and would probably have dropped the phone in shock when he explained!

Everything to do with the shop and healing centre seemed to be guided and effortless. I asked internally for help building the business and within a few days was woken and told that I needed to place an advert in the Matlock Mercury, the local newspaper. I mentioned it to Mum and before I had any chance to do anything about it, a young lady called at the shop to introduce herself. She was new in town and working for the Matlock Mercury. If we wanted to place an advert she would give us a discounted rate. I followed my insight and placed the advert. Naturally it had a good response.

I was also thinking about placing a small advert in 'Reflections', a good-quality magazine covering

Derbyshire. It was quite expensive at two hundred pounds for a relatively small black and white advert. I designed the advert and phoned to speak to someone about it. For some reason the editor answered the phone. He was fascinated about what I did and we ended up with a full-page colour article; all that free advertising with very little effort. Conversely, when I decided to place an advert, we got no response or a negligible response. I soon learned to place adverts only when guided to and the best advertising undoubtedly came from satisfied clients telling their friends.

One couple that called into the shop soon after it was first opened was particularly impressed. They were holidaying in Derbyshire and Shirley had been having quite a bit of back and leg trouble to the extent that she could only walk for a short distance before she needed the aid of a walking stick. The discomfort was putting a damper on their holiday because Shirley wasn't able to walk as far as she would like and they were used to being quite active. I offered her a healing. Shirley was quite sceptical but said she would give it a go. Her husband waited outside. The treatment lasted about an hour but at the end of it she no longer felt the need for her stick. Shirley and her husband were both so impressed that they wrote to the local paper about their experience and they both called in to see us whenever they were holidaying in the area. To the best of my knowledge Shirley didn't need to use her stick again. She joked that we should put a display of walking sticks, no longer needed by people, in the display cabinet outside the shop.

I never knew quite what kind of response I would get when I healed. I didn't know how the healing worked exactly. I only experienced that it did. There didn't seem to be anything I could do to make a healing work better, except relax fully. It made no difference whether the client believed in healing or was sceptical. Religious or spiritual beliefs similarly made no difference to the results. I just had to get my logical side out of the way and accept that whatever happened was the right thing.

Sometimes patients would feel lots happening during a healing and I wouldn't feel anything. At other times I would have profound physical feelings whilst doing the healing and the patient would feel nothing. Some healings that I expected to be successful weren't and at times healings that I didn't expect to be successful were. My logical brain couldn't make sense of it and after a while I just stopped trying to do so.

One of my most curious 'successes' was a gentleman with multiple sclerosis or MS. The MS was quite advanced and he needed two walking sticks to get about. If he continued to deteriorate he would soon be in a wheelchair and he was working hard to find a way to avoid that. After his first healing, there was only a small improvement and so as part of his second healing I asked what he needed to learn or understand before a full healing could be granted. I could have asked this internally myself but was wary that this would be disempowering. Patients need to understand how to access their own higher knowing. So I developed a technique where the patients could get in touch with their higher self and get their own answers.

This particular patient tried out the technique with me. He was told three things he needed to learn or understand. He relayed them to me one by one; to love himself, to forgive and to live in the present. When he returned home, much to his surprise, he found he could climb the stairs unaided and without difficulty. Unfortunately, by the morning all the MS symptoms had returned and he needed his sticks once more. Though his higher self had told him what he needed to learn, he still had to learn it and until he did he would have the MS symptoms.

It was another clear signal to me that I was not in charge of the healing; a higher power was. Successful healings were not really miracles; they were simply a working of natural law. If we understood the natural law that applied we would understand how to effect a healing. Mind, body and spirit are inexplicably intertwined and by working on one aspect you automatically affect the others. It was the beginning of my deeper realisation that the beliefs that we hold about reality and ourselves can affect us physically and how changing those beliefs either consciously or unconsciously can have profound effects on our physical body.

One of the healings that surprised me the most was on a young girl of about four. I had previously done healing on both of the girl's parents. It was her father who phoned me. He was really grateful for all I had done for him and he asked if it would be possible to try healing on his daughter. One of her legs was longer than the other and although it hadn't affected her too much so far she was just starting to develop a limp. He hardly dared hope that I would be able to help. I agreed to see her and made it clear that I may not be able to do anything at all.

When the young girl came in with her father, a stuffed toy reindeer in the healing room caught her eye. I decided to hold the reindeer by its feet as my hands moved over the various different places on her small body that they were guided to. This seemed to work, at least in that it helped her to feel more relaxed. The whole healing probably lasted about ten to fifteen minutes. I didn't feel much happening throughout, although I don't know whether it was because I was holding the reindeer or not.

Once I had been made aware that the healing was over, I asked the young girl if she had felt anything. "Tickling," she said. We stood her up, nothing seemed to have changed. As they left, her father thanked me for my time and said that it had been worth a try. About twenty minutes later, the phone rang. It was the girl's father phoning to thank me. He and his daughter were at home and the limp had gone. I was very surprised, as it hadn't felt as though it was a strong healing.

Word soon gets around a small town such as Matlock and so before long, we had a regular stream of clients. Two nurses, a doctor and a dentist also came in as clients and started recommending us to others, which helped our credibility no end.

Unfortunately, one of our neighbours wasn't so positive. Next door but one was a Christian bookshop and reports came back to us that they were praying for us; praying for us to leave. This was not a new thing. As I look back I have had lots of different people praying for me and praying for my soul. These people usually feel that what I am doing is somehow evil. The first time this occurred was at a show I organised for Vanessa. A group of very young 'Christians' came to 'save me'. I listened to them for over two hours. They clearly felt that mediumship was the work of the devil. When I went home that night I asked for guidance. I did not want to be doing anything 'wrong'. As I asked for help, I opened up a bible. There I read the story of Jesus going up a mountain and transfiguring into Moses and Elijah. I had never realised that Jesus had worked as a medium[3]. I felt reassured, since Jesus would not have done anything evil, and so I slept peacefully that night.

The next day brought with it an interesting turn of events. A young man, a committed Christian who regularly stood on street corners in Sheffield preaching to all who would listen, was brought to see me. He was a lovely young man. The young girl that brought him in was afraid that he was going to take his own life.

We chatted for a while and when he was comfortable he confided that he loved God with all his heart and he wanted to be a good Christian more than anything but in his heart-of-hearts he hated standing up and preaching to people. He couldn't see how he could be a good Christian if he didn't do the preaching. He just couldn't see a way forward.

I quietened my mind and asked for help. I found myself smiling internally and then externally. My mind became worried. Here was a young man baring his soul about how suicidal he was and I was smiling. Whatever my response was going to be, it had better be good, I thought to myself. It was.

"If God can get through to me," I said, "Don't you think God can get through to anyone? God doesn't require anyone to do His recruiting. He has direct access to every individual." The look of relief on the young man's face said it all. He was free to love his God, be a good Christian and not have to preach. I realised with hindsight that his visit to me was as much for my benefit as his as it confirmed that what I was doing was not in conflict with my own Christian-based beliefs. I was brought up as a Christian although not a churchgoing one, more one who did as Christ preached; treated others as I myself would like to be treated and loved others as myself. These are profoundly simple and yet profoundly powerful tenets for the way we should live our lives.

I consider that all the different religions are there for a purpose. I have, however, endeavoured to keep secular religion out of all that I do. People should be welcome to follow whatever religion they choose and to hold whatever beliefs they choose, but to me our humanity needs to come ahead of our ideology. If our beliefs serve us in becoming more loving, wise and peaceful people, that is great. If they don't, then perhaps we need to look at what we believe and why.

I did occasional readings at Inner Peace but most of my work was healing. Throughout my time there I experienced what I now call 'knowings'. One of the earliest occasions this happened for me, was in a private consultation when a lady asked me about her daughter. I saw, clairvoyantly, that the daughter had almost died when she was two. The lady, a sceptic, wanted to know what of and immediately I knew the daughter had suffered from a twisted colon. I didn't know how I knew, but I would have staked my life on it. It came straight out of my mouth and sure enough the lady confirmed I was correct. For most of us these kinds of 'knowings' bypass our rational-thinking left-brain.

Working at Inner Peace continued to bring many surprises. We would occasionally have young girls of perhaps thirteen or fourteen call into the shop wanting to buy books on 'witchcraft'. We didn't stock anything remotely like that and I was amazed to find how much 'witchcraft' was apparently going on and how many very young people were being drawn into it. I had always given anything to do with witchcraft a very wide berth but this level of interest made me feel the need to find out more, to know if it was something people needed to protect themselves and their children from.

When I attended the NFSH healing course with Jack and Jan Angelo I had been told a little about the Witchcraft Act, which was introduced in the sixteenth century to give the church control of the people. Many people who were then termed 'witches' were in fact what today we would call healers or herbalists. The church of the day felt that too many people were turning to these people rather than to the churches. To instil fear in the masses, an evil or dark image of witches was created which bore little resemblance to the reality.

Witchcraft, I found out, and I still have a very limited knowledge of it, was more to do with an appreciation of the seasons and the elements than flying around on broomsticks. White witchcraft involved casting spells for other people's benefit and black magic involved casting spells for your own benefit. Spells could range from what today we would call a positive affirmation such as, "I am healthy and whole.", to casting a spell on another person for your own personal benefit; cursing them in effect. I have never came across anyone using eye of newt or toe of bat.

I heard about several covens within the surrounding areas of Matlock and was checked out by at least one to see if I would be interested in joining them. It just wasn't for me. I recognised that I probably still had some fear about witchcraft, perhaps from my early programming during childhood. Was it unfounded? Who knows? It is just not a path I choose to explore in this lifetime. Whenever we had enquiries about witchcraft in the shop I found out what it was that the enquirer really wanted to know and then was able to point them in a direction with which I was more familiar.

At Inner Peace I spent many, many hours healing and listening, often in a meditative state. It was where I too found my inner peace and my inner piece. There were many lessons for me; patience, tolerance, openness and trust.

On a very practical level, however, I also had to learn a lot about money that I didn't previously know.

Money

The healing centre was developing an excellent reputation in Derbyshire, with referred clients coming from as far away as Scotland, but despite this we were only just managing to pay the bills.

Why was it that if I needed seventy-two pounds to pay a phone bill the shop would take seventy-two pounds exactly? If I needed two hundred and thirteen pounds we would take two hundred and thirteen pounds. This happened on a consistent basis; so consistent it was spooky! What was the universe trying to teach me? What was I trying to teach myself?

Somehow we just managed to stay within our overdraft facility. We always had enough to pay our bills, even if it meant juggling credit cards at times. I didn't understand it. All my working life I'd had plenty of money. I'd used a credit card but was able to clear it when I needed to. Now, all of a sudden, I had to watch what I spent money on. And it seemed the more I watched my spending, the worse my financial situation got. I would spend hours balancing the bank statements and preparing financial forecasts. The situation got no better and no worse.

I rebelled inside. I thought I was supposed to be taken care of! A part of me was angry about what was happening. I had given up a secure well-paid job to embark on this 'spiritual journey'. Why wasn't I being better taken care of?

The feedback I was getting from clients indicated that I was doing people tremendous good and yet here I was struggling to pay for groceries for the first time in my life. Surely this wasn't right? What was I missing?

There were times I really regretted being so keen to give up my well-paid job. I would dream about being back at the bank and then wake up to the realisation I had resigned. I even thought about going back, cap-in-hand, to ask for work, perhaps part-time work, but I couldn't. Something inside would not let me. Perhaps it was pride? No! It was something else. Bank work would be soul-destroying for me now. I knew too much about another dimension or side of life. There could be no going back.

There were no holidays and no treats. I couldn't even buy the make-up I liked, as it was too expensive. My hair got very long too as I would go as long as I possibly could before going to the hairdresser.

Thankfully I loved what I was doing. I felt, for the first time, that I was making a real difference in people's lives. I realised just how special it can be for someone to listen to another, especially for the older clients. Often nobody listened to them and it was great to see how such a simple thing would transform their whole outlook. In fact, I found that many of my clients of all ages had not been really listened to before. All they basically needed was a good listening to. Is it any wonder so many of us don't know what we want out of life when there is no one to listen to our thoughts as we think ourselves through life's journey? I realised that providing solely a listening service would have been very beneficial but along with the healing it was a very powerful combination.

Some clients needed touch, just a gentle hand on their shoulder and they would respond. I wondered just how many had no one to hug them and how the absence of this simple pleasure was affecting their health.

The Inner Peace business was steady but not booming, partly because our clients got better and didn't come back for further treatments and partly because if we realised a client couldn't really afford a treatment we didn't charge them. We weren't providing healing solely for the money and that was evidenced by our overdraft.

We were victims of our own success in many ways. It might be months before we saw our clients again and when they did return they told us how much better they had been after their healing, but that didn't help with paying the bills in between times.

I continued to wonder why I was in such a financial situation. I blamed myself for not starting the business while I was still in employment. In quiet moments I reflected on the bigger picture. Many of the other 'spiritual' people I knew were having financial problems too. Did taking a spiritual path mean you effectively had to give up the material side of life? I recollected that the Bible tells us, 'It is easier for a camel to pass through the eye of a needle than for a rich man to enter the kingdom of heaven'. Should I just accept that this was how my life was now and cut my cloth accordingly? I wasn't starving. My needs were being met, though only just. But deep inside I didn't accept that we were here to live in sackcloth and ashes. It just didn't feel right. Why was I having the financial experiences I was? Was it that I needed to be more grateful for what I did have?

I reflected on the people I had come across while working for the bank who were experiencing financial difficulties. What did they have in common? Firstly, they tended to blame something or someone else for their situation. Their car repair or bill was never expected, their employers never paid enough and groceries were always too expensive. They blamed their partner, their children, their employer, their bank, their accountant and the taxman; even the government. Helping them sort out their finances invariably meant getting them to take responsibility for the situation they had created. So how could I apply that to my situation?

I realised that I was blaming a past decision – leaving the bank – for all that was currently happening. I was spending lots of time and energy looking at what had happened in the past and where money had gone. I was spending even more time projecting finances into the future. Both activities were absolutely futile and stress-creating. You cannot change the past and the future may or may not happen in the way that you project. The future is created by the actions you take NOW.

Accepting responsibility for the situation meant looking at what was and then making conscious decisions about what I could do to change it there and then. What positive action could I take now? I could advertise, but the overdraft would not allow it. How could I promote the business for free? I came up with the idea of doing free talks and demonstrations. It would take a while for them to result in money coming in, however, so in the meantime I needed to reduce my outgoings.

My mum was also feeling financially stretched, so we pooled resources and lived together for a time until the business grew sufficiently to support us better. Slowly the business grew but I still knew there was something else I had to learn about money. What was that key?

Learning about money has been one of my key lessons this lifetime. There must have been some reason for me spending sixteen years working for a bank! I did learn about the mechanics of money at the bank; how to invest, property law, stocks and shares, the money markets and so on but I didn't learn how to become abundant. Why do some people earn more than others? It didn't necessarily have anything to do with how hard they worked. Money just came more easily to some people than others. It had always come easily to me, I decided, so why should it be any different now? What had changed? Looking back I can see precisely what had happened, but at the time I couldn't see the wood for the trees.

When I worked for the bank I always had the belief that I would be well paid and I was. I believed that each year I would earn more money and I did. I would run up a credit card and then repay it on a regular basis. When I stopped working for the bank and opened the healing centre I believed that all my needs would be met – and they were; to the exact pound!

What were limiting me were my beliefs. All I actually had to do was change my beliefs and my experience of reality would also change. Of course that can be easy or difficult depending on what you believe.

In meditation, I was given a further insight into what was happening. The teaching surprised me at first. It was all about the physical law of cause and effect. I had first heard about the law of cause and effect in physics classes at school; we push a glass off a table and it hits the ground and smashes. The cause is the act of pushing. The effect is the broken glass. Sometimes in life we are conscious of the chain of events; we know the pushed glass results in the broken glass. If we walk into a room and find broken glass on the floor we may not know the cause but we can use reason and logic to work out how the glass might have come to be broken. What I hadn't fully realised until that point was that the law of cause and effect also applies to our thoughts.

Many people would agree that if they left the house expecting to meet bad drivers on the road then this is what they would experience. Equally, if you think you are going to have a really difficult day you will and if you think you are going to meet an interesting stranger sometime in the next few days, you probably will.

Why then should it be any different where money is concerned? By examining my beliefs about money I started to realise exactly where I was limiting myself and holding myself back. I was told that there are no limitations except the ones we place on ourselves either consciously or unconsciously. A cluster of beliefs about abundance was what had created my experience of money and these beliefs included my sense of unworthiness. As soon as I released and dismissed my blocks to abundance, the universe would reflect this back to me through increased abundance.

So all that was happening was the universe was mirroring back to me what I believed about money and abundance. The universe wasn't judging my beliefs as right or wrong, it wasn't saying how much money I deserved to have. The universe was pointing out cause and effect to me. The universe is impartial about how much we have. What is important is that while we are here in physical form we learn how our thoughts affect our reality. Once I understood the theory, it felt as though I was being patted on the back.

I put it into my own words to check that I did have the teaching correct. I already knew that when I thought positive thoughts, I perceived what happened to me in my life in a more positive light. I now understood that I could either be at 'cause' in my life or at 'effect'. When you are at 'effect', life happens to you. This perspective leaves you feeling powerless as though there is nothing you can do about the situation.

By seeing yourself as at 'cause', however, you recognise that you are wholly responsible for all that happens to you, either individually or as part of the mass consciousness and you therefore know that you have the power to change the situation. The beauty of it is that you don't need to know precisely how you created the present situation; you only need to acknowledge that at some level you did and be prepared to let go of the beliefs you currently hold.

The universe was showing me that the unconscious beliefs I held, created the effects I was experiencing. By bringing those beliefs into consciousness, that is, by becoming aware of them, I could choose to continue to hold those beliefs about money or change to some different beliefs. If I changed my beliefs or even just let go of the ones I was holding onto so tightly, I would experience a different reality. I was happy that I understood the theory. Now it was time to try it out in practice.

Day by day I started to experiment with my beliefs and to notice what feedback I got from the universe. Some days I got it more right than others and some days I almost seemed to go backwards. I learned to lighten up and not take the whole issue too seriously. It was almost like playing a game with the universe. The universe seemed to be testing me to see if I had really changed my beliefs or if I would go back to the old ways of blaming someone or something for my situation. It took some time but I could feel myself making progress and little by little increased abundance came my way. I was starting to learn about abundance at last and what surprised me was that the new way of being took less energy and effort than the old way. And it was fun! In my old way of thinking I held beliefs about how I could generate money and these were limited to my experience of earning money to date. In my new way of being I knew absolutely that I was connected to the 'All That Is' and through being me and doing what I truly loved to do I both increased my energy and expanded my energy field. In this new expanded way of being I could not help but flow more abundance through me and into my life.

During this time I also experienced a lack of clients from time to time. I didn't understand it. Why, when I did such amazing healing was the world not beating a path to my door? I had much to learn, not least of which was humility. Yes, the healings were very often amazing, but I was only ever an instrument, a channel. I didn't understand what was happening let alone have any power to affect it. Some people would get amazing healings and some wouldn't and it had nothing to do with me. I had no say in what happened. The healing was clearly not of me but through me. My focus was to keep myself 'clear' which I did by meditating, relaxing and thinking loving thoughts. Stress and healing do not go together.

Very often I found I could not answer clients' questions about a healing. I didn't understand how it worked or why it worked or if the healing would be permanent, although it nearly always was. Not knowing how the healing worked, or whether it would, helped me keep my feet on the ground. It stopped my ego from running away with me. Humility is a strange quality. When you think you have it, you no longer do! No sooner had I worked through the humility lesson than I found myself staring at my next lesson in the mirror.

A red patch had appeared on my face. It was a perfect circle. At first I thought it was dry skin but over the next few days a second circle appeared and then a third. All were perfect circles and from what I could tell it looked a lot like ringworm. I hadn't seen it before but Mum had. She was pretty sure it was ringworm, but had never seen it on someone's face before. I didn't like to go to doctors, so I tried to diagnose myself from a medical book. I had tried healing myself using the healing energies but there seemed to be a block. Weeks passed. It wouldn't respond to anything 'natural'. It didn't get any worse but it didn't get any better either and so in the end I admitted defeat and went to see a doctor, a rare experience for me.

Yes, it was definitely ringworm, but the doctor confirmed it was very unusual to get it on the face. I was prescribed a steroid cream to apply twice a day. I did not like the idea of using steroid cream on my face, especially as I read in the accompanying leaflet that it was, 'likely to thicken the skin'. I quickly decided I had better get to the cause of the ringworm through going within.

It took quite a while to uncover and then release the cause; unworthiness. I was feeling unworthy of my abilities or gifts as some people would call them. I was feeling unworthy of what it was I was here to do. The ringworm had manifested on my face because it was time to face up to these feelings, recognise them and deal with them. I recognised that it was also linked with my issues to do with abundance on which I had recently been working. It took several weeks to work through all of the issues. Finally my internal guidance told me, "Just by being here you do what you came here to do; opening to love and light. It is only the ego that says you have to do a certain thing. Nothing is required of you. You already are all that you need to be. Do whatever you do with an open, loving heart and do it because you want to. Do it knowing that whether or not you do it you are still loved." As soon as I had worked through those issues, the ringworm disappeared and has not returned since.

It was not long before I was tested again to see if I would use my abilities as a medium. A gentleman called at the shop. He had heard that I was able to talk to spirit world. He wanted to know if I would help him to contact his deceased wife. I said I would give it a try. It was a while since I had worked as a medium. His wife came through easily and clearly and I was able to give her name and other good evidence to prove whom she was. I was glad to be working as a medium again. Giving evidence that shows a loved one is still here can be profoundly healing to those left behind as it was in this case. It was a wonderful session and triggered many tears for both my client and myself.

The following week I was surprised to see the same gentleman's name in the appointment book. When the appointment time came around he wanted to talk with his wife again. It was unusual to see someone twice like that but I put it down to him needing more reassurance. When he tried to book for a third time it didn't feel right. We talked about what was happening and why he felt the need to come in again. He missed his wife dreadfully and could only feel close to her when he came in for a consultation with me. I explained how concerned I was that he was effectively becoming dependent on me and that it would be far better for him to communicate with his wife direct.

He said that he would love to do that and asked whether I could help him to learn how. "Of course!" came out of my mouth and I agreed to see him the following week to start teaching him how. I immediately regretted what I had said. What if I couldn't teach him how to do it? What if he didn't have the ability? When I got home I decided to ask for help and immediately got the response, "Whatever you imagine you can do, you can." So I chose to imagine that I would be able to get him to see, sense and hear his wife in one lesson.

The day of the first lesson arrived and I was quite nervous. I knew the gentleman was coming with high hopes; hopes that I had encouraged. I asked for help again and as much as I could, I let a higher power guide me in the process. Within ten minutes he was able to see, sense and hear his wife. Tears rolled down his cheeks and down mine. He didn't need me after that. He could talk to her whenever he wished.

There was much time for introspection and meditation at Inner Peace and my time there was time well spent. I learnt much about myself and as I aligned my life increasingly with my truth, I felt more at peace. As I felt more at peace, love started to bubble up inside of me. I was really starting to find my 'inner piece' as well as my 'inner peace' and it would only get better.

Choosing a Partner

Finances at the centre were at last starting to improve and I was beginning to feel in need of a holiday. In the three years since opening the business it would be my first. As a bank manager I was used to having three holidays a year, but I hadn't missed them until now.

I really needed a proper holiday and soon. Mum and I shopped around for a bargain. A friend, Rebecca, was keen to join us and in no time at all the three of us found ourselves in the sun at one of the Canary Islands.

The days were hot and lazy and centred on the pool. I was feeling very peaceful, very happy and very in control of my life. Perhaps now would be a good time to think about having another relationship I thought. I played around with the idea for a while. It was almost two years since Manos and I had separated. I was thirty-four and the years were passing by. Perhaps I should request a 'significant other-half'.

Since awakening psychically and spiritually three years previously I had met so many women keen, and occasionally desperate, to meet partners and I reflected now on how they did and why they didn't meet partners. Several had carried the belief that all men were unfaithful and yet they wanted to meet a partner who would be faithful. Of course they continued to meet partners who were unfaithful. Their first belief that 'all men are unfaithful' won, and created their experience of reality. Looking at their lives clairvoyantly I could see what needed to change. I helped them to consciously change whatever was blocking them and so create a future where they drew to themselves a loyal partner. If they exercised their free will choice and allowed their belief that 'all men were unfaithful' to persist, there was nothing that I was able to do.

Some women honestly expected to be able to sit at home and magically meet 'Mr Right'. Did they expect him to knock on their door? Some women were too desperate and too needy. You did not need to be psychic to see how they would scare the men away. I remember one lady, who was very keen to find a partner but definitely didn't want him to be English. Why then, live in England? It was bizarre. Women would tell me they wanted one thing and then be taking action that flew directly in the face of what they said they wanted.

A great many believed in the concept of soul mates, perhaps encouraged by fairy tales and romantic stories, perhaps sometimes because another psychic had told them about a dark-haired gentleman that would sweep them off their feet in years to come. Personally, I had never believed in soul mates as such. It always seemed so disempowering. What if they died? Imagine the pain of losing your one and only soul mate? I had seen some clients who were in this mindset and I had felt their pain. 'Why choose that for yourself?' I thought. 'Why choose a way of looking at the world that creates pain?'

What if your so-called 'soul mate' didn't even know you existed, or was married to someone else? Or what if they didn't wake up spiritually and you did? It would cause huge pain and it didn't make sense to me that life would be like that.

From what I had experienced in my own life and seen clients experience in theirs, it seemed more likely that there are several people who are on your wavelength at any one time. Inside, we all have a frequency or essence and this essence vibrates at a particular resonance. Depending on how we are resonating we pull towards us what we most need at any one time in much the same way as magnets pull and repel one other. If one person pulls away from us and our relationship with them ends, there are many more there ready to be pulled towards us if that is what we most need for our highest good. I had noticed that there were times that I needed relationships and times that I needed to be alone. It depended on what I was working on. Now I was ready for a relationship, it would be a perfect time to put my theories about relationships to the test.

Lying at the side of the pool, I decided that I didn't want to pull just anyone to me, it had to be a special someone, a significant other. I went within and checked that all parts of me were ready to connect with someone and made my list of how I would like him to be; open, honest, successful, a good communicator, sensual, romantic, good-looking, confident, caring, ready to commit, healthy, no children, fun and so the list went on. It was a long list. I tried not to miss anything out. If you are going to do this and you have the whole universe to choose from you might as well do it properly. I then mentally intended myself to meet this person, harming no one else in the process and for the good of all. Adding that phrase ensures that what you intend is for everyone's highest good. If you don't, it's a little bit like witchcraft.

"And what would you give to the relationship?" asked my higher-level guidance. I started to make a list, but was stopped and referred back to my previous list. I was asked whether I was also equally prepared to give the same qualities that I had wanted from this new partner. For the first time in thirty-four years, I realised that always in relationships I had focused on what I was getting rather than what I was giving. It was a 'light bulb moment' for me. I suddenly saw this as the main reason why I worked with so many people who were dissatisfied with their relationships. They were all focusing on what they were getting or not getting rather than what they were giving. Over time if you focus purely on what you are getting, the flow of energy between the two of you will diminish until there is nothing left. If you focus though on what you are giving, relationships often get increasingly meaningful and flourish. It is so simple.

All I had to do was focus on what I was now prepared to give. I went through the list and, after some internal debate, agreed that I was in fact ready to give all that I had wanted from a new partner.

That night as I went to sleep I had a vivid dream. I was shown my next partner and that a particular shade of green would be significant. In the dream, my new partner wanted to buy me a drink, a beer. In real life I never let anyone buy me a drink, and I didn't drink beer, but in the dream I was shown it was safe to let him buy a drink for me. Dreams are often symbolic rather than literal so I didn't pay it much attention.

The next evening, sitting in the pool bar a Spanish man tried to get my attention. I ignored him to begin with and then was quite rude. I did not want a holiday romance. He persisted and I indicated that I really wasn't interested, although I had to award him ten out of ten for perseverance. He spoke English but with that London accent you get when you learn English overseas or from cassette tapes or so I thought.

He came over to sit with me, much to my discomfort and for the first time I noticed he was wearing a green jumper in precisely the shade of green I had been shown in my dream. He told me he was English, but I wasn't convinced. I still thought he was Spanish. And then he told me he was a doctor and that he had taught himself to speak Spanish. I didn't believe a word of it, but as we talked more I came to the reluctant and embarrassed conclusion that he was in fact English, that he was a doctor. It turned out green was his favourite colour. He warned me that if ever I saw where he lived, and he was about to move into a new flat, I would see that nearly everything would be green.

"How come you are holidaying here?" I asked, making polite conversation.

" I'm not sure really," he replied. "About midday yesterday I suddenly had this urge to go into a travel agent's and book a trip away. This is where I ended up."

I nearly spat out my drink. The timing was spookily close to the time I had put out my intent to the universe. Here he was in the flesh, less than thirty-six hours later! I did hope I had put everything I wanted on my list!

As it turned out I wasn't disappointed. Our friendship grew, we found we had a lot in common and an incredible relationship developed out of it. It was marred, however, by one thing; his total disbelief in what I did. For some reason I had not thought to require an acceptance of things spiritual when I made my list of desirable qualities for a new partner. We got on fine as long as I did not talk about what I did or what I believed.

When we both returned to the UK, I was introduced to his parents. I was only the second girl he had taken to meet his parents so I knew his feelings towards me were genuine. He introduced me to his parents as, 'an ex-bank manager who now has her own business running a gift shop'. He mentioned nothing about the healing I did or talking to the dead. And I understood that reaction because of the nature of my work.

I didn't talk to him too much about my trip to India to see Sai Baba either, which was just a few weeks away. How would I explain Sai Baba and my need to visit him to someone who was obviously a sceptic? I couldn't even explain Sai Baba to myself. After first hearing about Sai Baba at Stephen Turoff's healing centre I had been curious to find out more but I couldn't remember his name. Then, more than a year later I spotted a photo of Sai Baba in a room at Alison Harper's development circle. The distinctive orange robe and afro hair were unmistakable. Eventually I had found a book about Sai Baba in a New Age bookstore. It was called 'Embodiments of Love', by Peggy Mason and Ron Laing. The book was two parts in which first Ron and then Peggy describe their own personal experiences of Sri Sathya Sai Baba.

Sai Baba defines himself as an Avatar; which is to say a divine incarnation. Specifically, he describes himself as a Purnavatar, or an incarnation of God with all his complete powers. He describes himself as God and also goes on to say that, "You too are God, the only difference is that you do not know it yet." Sai Baba's ashram is called Prasanthi Nilayam (Abode of Great Peace) and is in Puttaparthi in Southern India. Days at the ashram revolve around an event known as 'darshan,' (sight of the Lord) when Sai Baba walks through an open-air, pastel-coloured hall called a mandir. Darshan takes place once in the very early morning and once in the afternoon and people from around the world line up for hours beforehand to be part of it. The ashram accommodates as many as 30,000 people at one time. On special occasions such as Christmas and Sai Baba's birthday even more are accommodated. Many Indian people just sleep on the ground. There is a special chamber for private interviews and every day Sai Baba selects a handful of devotes to join him privately. It is during these private interviews, or inner-views as he calls them, that Sai Baba does most of his famous materialisations, ostensibly conjuring up objects like rings, watches, necklaces and vibhutti (sacred ash) from the air as gifts for his devotees.

'Embodiments of Love' takes its title from the way in which Sai Baba often addresses devotees as embodiments of love. It was the only book I could find on Sai Baba for quite a long time and so I eventually wrote to the authors for more information. I was delighted to receive a handwritten response from Peggy, one of the authors, almost by return post. Peggy explained that her husband Ron had passed over since writing the book. Her letter went on to say that she received a great many letters each day and I was touched that Peggy had taken the time and trouble to respond to mine. Peggy was editor of a quarterly publication that told stories about Sai Baba and for a small fee, to cover printing and postage she would add me to her mailing list. It seemed like a good way of finding out more about Sai Baba. After all, if there was a Christ on the planet, you would want to find out more wouldn't you?

The quarterly magazines arrived and were a nice little read full of inspiring stories, but I wasn't really drawn to Sai Baba as a teacher. Sai Baba didn't look at all like I would expect a Christ to look and the stories of materialising jewellery and gifts for devotees put me off somewhat. For a start, I wanted a Christ to at least look like a Christ though he did have very nice loving eyes.

It took me by completely by surprise one day after reading the quarterly magazine, to suddenly feel compelled to go to see Sai Baba. I even knew which group I had to go with. I had no spare money but I was so certain that I was meant to go that I put the cost of the airfare, six hundred pounds, on my credit card. As a business owner this was not something I would ordinarily do. Money was tight enough and I had no real means of repaying the debt but I knew I had to go. I didn't even check with my mum who I would need to leave to look after the shop. I just had to go. I would have closed the shop if I'd had to. Mum was happy to cover for me but worried that I might be getting into some kind of a cult, and who could blame her. If Sai Baba had this much pull over me from the other side of the world, how would he affect me when I stayed at the ashram?

On Tuesday at 7:30 in the morning of the week I was due to fly to India, there was a knock at my door.

It was a tax inspector. I had never even had a letter or phone call from a tax inspector, let alone had one arrive on my doorstep at 7:30 in the morning. He had some questions about my previous year's accounts. He couldn't understand why I would have given up such a well-paid job to be now earning so little. It didn't make sense to him.

We went through my year's accounts together and it turned out I had made a simple mistake with them in the tax department's favour. The tax inspector was happy with my explanation, asked me if I would like to reclaim some of the tax I had paid as a bank manager and offered to look into it for me. By Saturday, the day I was due to fly to India, there was a cheque on my doormat for almost two thousand pounds. Have you ever known the Inland Revenue Department to repay you money within forty-eight hours? I took it that the universe was supporting my trip to see Sai Baba. I travelled to India as part of an organised tour with a group which I considered would be much easier than trying to arrange everything by myself, especially as I did not speak the local language, Telgu.

Janet and Peter were our trip leaders and excelled at their role. They organised an initial introductory afternoon in their home for us all to meet one other before we left which assured us that we would not be travelling alone. They also eased our concerns about what life on the ashram would be like. They explained that there were three kinds of accommodation; some visitors shared rooms with bathroom facilities for three to five people, shared family accommodation, and then some huge dormitories where one hundred and fifty to two hundred men or women slept with just suspended sheets between one another. The sexes were strictly segregated unless people were married. We all hoped we would get the first kind of accommodation but there could be no promises. We would get what was available.

We could hire beds for just a few rupees. Indian food would be served, but there was a western-style cafeteria where the Indian food was milder and catered more for the western palate. We were warned to be sure to take plenty of electrolytes, enough for the whole trip of three weeks, in case of diarrhoea. Living costs would be negligible by western standards, a mere two or three pounds a day and so spending money of just two hundred pounds was suggested. Sai Baba encouraged visitors to spend as much time as possible in the ashram rather than in the shops! He was concerned about how the visitors with their apparent wealth affected the people in the surrounding area.

By the time the trip came around I was ready to go. Janet and Peter had suggested some more books about Sai Baba to read and had given us a booklet about life on the ashram, which answered most of my questions.

It was quite a long flight to India with a change of planes en route. I wasn't sitting with anyone I knew and so there was time for me to reflect and meditate. I remember two significant insights during the flight. The first insight was how your thoughts, whatever they are, go out into the universe forever. They don't stop inside your head. They go out into the space around you and keep on going outwards where others can pick them up. I decided I had better start watching my thoughts more, and my feelings for that matter. For a split second I understood completely about the interconnectedness of all things. I understood why the law of cause and effect is as it is; all is interconnected. We might not see the connections with our physical eyes but those connections are nevertheless still there in much the same way as we feel the love between another and ourselves.

The second insight was about poverty. I had heard that the begging situation in India was particularly bad with some Indians maiming their newborn children so that people would pity them and so give them more money. The insight explained that by giving money to someone who is begging, you reinforce their belief that they need to beg. When you give them money, you affirm to them that you consider that they are incapable of earning money or supporting themselves in any other way. You are, in effect, agreeing with their limited perception of themselves and by doing so you help keep them in poverty. I decided not to give to beggars any more but instead to try to help people to help themselves. I didn't know it then but very soon I would be tested on this.

India

I had never been to India before so really had no idea of what to expect. We arrived in Bangalore, India, at 2:30 in the morning after an arduous seven hour journey on two planes. I think we were all tired when we finally disembarked the second plane. Even though it was very early morning there were already quite a few people milling around the airport and I couldn't help but notice the clouds of mosquitoes that engulfed us as we walked through the main concourse. I was glad I had covered myself with mosquito repellent on the plane. Some of the other passengers were not so lucky and were bitten quite badly. The locals seemed totally immune both to the clouds of mosquitoes and to being bitten.

We were all weary as we made our way out of the airport after collecting our luggage. I remember noticing the smell of the night air. It was warm and different to anything I had smelled before, though neither pleasant nor unpleasant. Taxis had been ordered to take us to our hotel. They were the oldest taxis I had ever seen but really solid. I didn't know vehicles this old still ran.

It was a short drive to our hotel. We spent our first night in India in what by Indian standards was a luxury five star hotel, although to most Europeans it was very basic accommodation. We shared rooms, with three or four people to a room. The bathroom consisted of two large plastic buckets. The idea was to crouch in one while using the other to pour water over yourself, but at least there was clean running water, which in itself exceeded my expectations. It was good to lie down to sleep after the long journey. It was very warm but the beds were comfortable and the linen was clean. Unlike most of the others, who found the room too hot, I slept well that night.

The next morning it was our first opportunity to see Bangalore in daylight, as trips into town were organised. Bangalore was a busy, dirty city with very different modes of transport and much older vehicles than I was used to seeing. There were a great many bikes and a strange kind of vehicle that was like a cross between a car and a bike. I was fascinated by how many vehicles there were on the roads and by their drivers' complete disregard for road rules or the personal safety of others. I couldn't believe just how many people were crammed into some vehicles, especially trucks. It had to be seen to be believed. The noise of horns beeping and people shouting was something I had not previously experienced.

The terracotta earth, was totally new to me; it struck me profoundly, confirming that I was in a different place. I had always thought earth was earth-coloured wherever you went.

The main purpose of the shopping trip was to buy suitable clothing for the ashram (the compound). Women could choose between saris or salwar kameez, which are trousers with a long top over them. Women needed to ensure their bodies were fully covered at all times in the ashram. Only your head and ankles were allowed to show. We would also need to wear a scarf at all times that identified us to our group and to our country.

Many of the salwar kameez suits were rather plain but the sari fabrics were beautiful and luxurious. I really quite liked the idea of wearing saris rather than the salwar kameez suits, as there were so many different fabrics and colours that it was hard to choose. Eventually I chose two saris, one in maroon, black and gold and the other in green and gold. Both were made in silk. I also purchased matching sari blouses, sort of cropped T-shirts, to wear underneath the saris.

The experience of shopping was something else. Child beggars were everywhere and if you gave them anything they simply didn't leave you alone. I watched the problems some of my travelling companions were having after giving money to them. If you said, "No!" from the start they still begged but were nowhere near as persistent. Once you had given something, they thought they could get more out of you and followed you wherever you went. I was grateful for the insight I'd had on the plane.

Back at the hotel, plans were being made for us all to have dinner together. In the interim the Indian women who were members of the group helped the rest of us to get to grips with putting on a sari. A sari is a strip of fabric, the length of which is about three times your physical height. In different parts of India the women wear their saris slightly differently. We had to learn the local way. You start by wrapping it around your waist and pleating it in a certain way so that you can move and sit down comfortably in it. Westerners tend to use safety pins to hold the pleats in place while the Indians are usually so skilled that they don't need to use anything. After pleating the fabric, you then wrap it across your chest and over your arm.

Putting on a sari is much harder than it looks. I decided to have some more practice after dinner and was able to get someone to agree to help me. I was finally feeling confident when another group member came in to say, "You do know that you will have to learn to do that in the dark and without a mirror, don't you? At the ashram we will be getting up at 3am and it will be pitch black." I had to learn to put the sari on by feel! How I wished I had bought the salwar kameez suits and that vanity had not got the better of me!

It was our last night in 'luxury'. Those of us in the group who had not previously visited the ashram were starting to get anxious about what lay in store, and especially the four hour taxi ride to the ashram which awaited us the next morning. The stories we heard about previous trips did not inspire confidence. Our tour guides had booked taxis for us with what was considered a reputable taxi firm but even the tour guides started to worry when all of our taxis failed to show up. It was a hot day and we did our best to stay in the shade as we waited. Eventually they arrived more than an hour and a half late and our guides bundled us into them in groups of four. There was a last minute warning not to expect too much from the toilets along the way.

The taxis were old and dusty, and the drivers were completely fearless; some would say reckless. We had been told that the journey would take several hours and that there would be just one stop along the way. When we made that stop, we understood what our guides meant when they said not to expect too much of the toilets. What toilets? It was a toilet in name only, better described as a hole and there was no toilet paper. The Indian custom is to use the hand. One hand is used at the toilet and the other for eating with. I decided I could hold on. I also decided not to eat in the cafe. It turned out to be a wise decision as those who did were ill by the evening.

Two more hours remained until we would be at the ashram. Our taxi rolled on. The windows were non-existent, which was just as well as the air-conditioning was non-existent too. We knew we were starting to draw close to the ashram when we started to see homes at the side of the road. The anticipation of seeing the ashram was starting to build. I had seen photos but photos often cannot capture the feeling of a place and it was the feeling of the ashram that affected me most profoundly when we finally arrived.

The taxis dropped us at the main entrance. We assembled our group, making sure we were all wearing our group scarves. As I walked in, I felt as though I was being held in a loving embrace. It felt as though an invisible pair of man's arms were around me, holding me and hugging me. I thought perhaps it was my imagination and focused instead on what I was seeing; the ashram buildings and all the people. But that feeling was still there, whether I paid it attention or not and I retained it until the day I left. The ashram felt overwhelming. People of many different nations were there although predominantly the devotees were Indian. The ashram buildings were aesthetically pleasing in pale pastel colours with occasional gold trim and the wonderful smell of fresh jasmine filled the air.

Once inside the ashram our guides took our passports to the central office to check us in and secure our accommodation. We were all excited and wondered what accommodation we would get. It was very hot and there was no shade. We waited. And we waited. Some of the children with the group were getting restless. Still we waited. We waited for three hours before seeing our guides again. The news was not good. We thought we had got the large block accommodation but it was worse than that! There was no accommodation, even for the families with children.

The guides talked us through our options. We could each individually try for accommodation in the town outside the ashram or we could wait and hope to get something. We waited in the heat, without shade, for another two hours until eventually our prayers were answered. Two of the families in our group managed to get into the family block. The rest of us were in the segregated large block accommodation. But now we were grateful for it! Our passports were returned to us and we made our way to what would be our 'home' for the next few weeks.

The large blocks were one huge warehouse-type room. String was hung from the ceiling and sheets were then hung from the string to form temporary walls between the inhabitants. We walked around and couldn't see quite where we were going to fit. A Seva Dal (ashram official) accompanied us and cleared some space. Some people were taking up far too much room apparently, although you couldn't tell just by looking. You had a space for your bed and then a space half that size to get dressed in and store your possessions. Accommodation was tight as it was and we were obviously unwelcome newcomers. We might not understand the language but we could certainly recognise not being welcome.

A woman called Tracey from the group I was travelling with, who was roughly my age, suggested we put our beds together and then share a double space for changing in. It sounded good to me. She had been to the ashram a couple of times before and so offered to go and get the beds while I hung the sheets and mosquito nets. The beds were very basic, consisting of a low, metal spring base and a thin, lumpy mattress. Our beds had to go right up against each other, which felt very odd with a complete stranger but Tracey was not a stranger for long. She had come to the ashram with her partner Neil, but they weren't allowed in the family quarters even had there been room for them, because they weren't married. I don't know why, but for some reason we began discussing how old we were and discovered that we were the same age, not just to the year or even to December, the month of our birth. The date of our birth was December 13th of the same year. With thirty thousand people at the ashram I found myself lying next to someone who was born on the exact same day as me, in the same year! I had never met anyone born on the same day as me before. The hairs on my arms stood on end.

After seeing the beds, Tracey's complete with bedbugs, I was totally amazed to find real working showers with hot and cold running water at the far end of the room. The five-star hotel hadn't even had these. Also, there were real toilets that you could sit on and flush. As I went to sleep that night I was truly grateful and decided that perhaps this Sai Baba could perform miracles after all.

It was still dark when alarms started going off in the block, the earliest at just 3:00 am and ours at 3:30. I was so excited about my first darshan (sight of the Lord) that I was keen to get out of bed. It was time to put on the sari but there was not a hope. No way could I put it on correctly in the dark without a mirror. Tracey came to my rescue and I was ready in time to meet the rest of the group to meditate and pray before going into darshan.

If you get to darshan early enough, you can sit in what are called lines, which are rows of men or women sitting cross-legged. These lines are then allocated numbers and the numbers are called to determine how close to Sai Baba you get to sit. If you arrive too late and you miss the lines you end up sitting at least twenty rows back. The Seva Dal are very good at organising the lines and the large numbers of people that visit the ashram. It was just our first darshan and yet we drew line two which meant the second row! Everyone was ecstatic and the excitement was almost tangible. We had just arrived and for us to get line two was very auspicious. We must surely get a group interview, we thought.

We sat a while longer before being called to our place in the mandir (main building). Once in the mandir you are expected to be completely quiet and pray or meditate until Baba appears. Many people though, are too excited so in truth the mandir only falls silent as Baba finally appears. During a darshan, Baba walks from his house into the mandir and then through the mandir. As he walks through he selects people for a group interview in a separate building. Once he has finished he walks back through the mandir to his house. A darshan typically lasts fifteen minutes though the wait is about three and a half hours in total time. Nonetheless, I always found it well worth the wait and never missed a darshan.

At my first darshan, Sai Baba looked straight at me and asked, "Why are you here?" except that his lips didn't move; I just heard the words in my head. Why was I there? I wasn't sure about Sai Baba and I was curious about who he was. I wanted to find out more. Was he truly a Christ or the Christ? I thought long and hard about what proof I would like and I decided that I wanted to be able to see his aura. What that would prove to me I didn't know, but that was what I asked for.

Throughout my three week stay at the ashram I would often hear Sai Baba talking to me in my head. I was also dreaming about him at night. According to the books I had read on Sai Baba it was not possible to dream about him without his consent. This had confirmed itself to me before my trip when I consistently tried to dream about him, but never managed to. My dreams at the ashram were always very vivid and always along the lines of surrender. In each dream Baba would encourage me to surrender and each time something inside wouldn't let me so I couldn't. I didn't know how to surrender, or how to let go. I didn't know then that it would take me five years to learn that particular lesson. My resistance was a natural phenomenon. We know at a deep level internally that we should not give our power away to anyone. Our enlightenment or spiritual advancement never rests on another person outside of ourselves. All we need is within. It would be a long five years before I eventually realised that surrender is an internal process. We surrender to a higher aspect of ourselves within, not to someone else outside of us.

The longest anyone is permitted to stay at the ashram in a year is four weeks, which helps to ensure that a cult mentality does not develop, a common-sense approach that I was reassured by. Our stay was for three weeks and the darshans were the highlight of my stay. At one particular darshan I decided to use my time waiting in the mandir to send distant healing to clients and friends in the UK. Usually when I sent distant healing I felt the energy come in through my head and out through my hands but instead this time it came in through my 'heart centre' and out through my hands. I opened my eyes in surprise and there in front of me was Baba. He had come into the mandir and I hadn't noticed. The healing energy was coming directly from him to me, or so it felt.

Throughout the stay, a series of incredible synchronous events took place, not only for me, but also for other members of the group. For example, Vijay, a young Indian man who was part of my group had been a devotee for many years and was particularly excited about seeing Baba. During darshan devotees would hold out to Baba their letters with requests in them. If he took your letter of request, the requests were granted and if he didn't they weren't. Vijay was keen to give Baba a letter and tried to get close at every opportunity. Eventually the opportunity arose and Vijay was able to lean across people and pass Baba a letter. Baba took his letter and immediately dropped it on the floor. Baba said, "Pick it up, pick it up." and the young man two rows in front of Vijay sitting at Baba's feet just froze and didn't pick up the letter, which just stayed on the floor.

Vijay was distraught. The request in his letter was selfless and really important to him and he wanted to know what it meant that Baba had dropped the letter and whether his request had been accepted or declined. Had Baba actually taken the letter, did it fall before it reached his hand or was it deliberately dropped? Why didn't the person in front just pick it up? Had Baba intentionally moved on without the letter? Vijay's mind was working overtime and I really felt for him.

Fortunately Vijay didn't have to suffer for long. At lunch he found himself sitting next to a young man who was telling his story about Baba. The young man had arrived in India just the night before. His flight had been delayed, the food on the plane had been awful, the seat was uncomfortable and draughty and so he had spent most of the flight and the subsequent evening mentally running down Air India. He went to his very first darshan and as Baba came past, a letter with an Air India plane pictured on it, landed at his feet. Baba had immediately known all of the man's negative thoughts and the man was mortified. Baba had asked the man to pick up the letter but he just froze and couldn't do so. "Pick it up. Pick it up." Baba had said and yet the man could not move. In the man's opinion, Baba had known how negative he had been feeling and Baba was telling him to pick up his thoughts.

Vijay's letter had been written on an Air India aerogramme and was the envelope that had dropped at his dining colleague's feet. At last Vijay was able to confirm with the young man that Baba had indeed taken his letter. Together they worked out that the letter had only been dropped for the young man's benefit and out of 30,000 people, Vijay and the young man happened to sit together for lunch that day! Vijay was feeling truly blessed.

It seemed everyone had a story to tell. One morning I noticed that an American lady and her two young children in our group were drinking the water straight out of the ashram taps rather than buying bottled water as the rest of the group did. At the first opportunity I decided to ask her about this. She explained that she felt that if Baba was God, or Godlike, then surely the water would be okay to drink and so she tried it first of all herself and then let her two children drink it. They had all been fine. It seemed a reasonable enough argument and I was keen to try the water for myself, albeit with some trepidation. It was absolutely fine, tasting better than tap water in the UK. I excitedly shared my new discovery with a number of my travelling companions although many still didn't trust it and stuck with the bottled water.

It was an amazing three weeks. The days were spent waking early, meditating, going to darshan and waiting for Sai Baba. This was our routine morning and afternoon. I loved every minute at the ashram and only ventured beyond it a couple of times. One such occasion was an organised trip to see the specialty hospital that Baba had established which provided the local community with free medical treatment and operations. I was impressed by both the fabulous architecture and with how the place felt; not like a hospital but like a place of healing. I wondered why it is that our western hospitals don't feel like this.

A small group of us went shopping just to experience life beyond the ashram walls. It wasn't long before I was accosted by one of the market stallholders.

"You English? You English?" he enquired with a heavy Indian accent. I nodded. "You rich lady! You take this boy home with you!" he urged. My attention was drawn to an attractive Indian boy of about eight or nine, who was standing just to the side of the stallholder. "He has no mother, no father! You take?" he persuaded. I was perplexed. He was asking me to take the boy. "What are you saying Dad?" asked the young boy pulling on his father's shirt. The stallholder was asking me to take his son. Here I was in India, on the other side of the world, visiting Sai Baba in the hope of finding something and here on Sai Baba's doorstep was an Indian man who desperately wanted what I had. He perceived I had what he wanted. I perceived that Indian spiritual people had what I wanted. I didn't know whether to laugh or cry. Later, in private, I cried. I cried for myself and my desperate searching, I cried for the small Indian boy whose father thought he would be better off with me, a 'rich Westerner' than with his own family and I cried for the Indian man who didn't realise how much he already had.

My stay at the ashram brought with it many new experiences. I tasted green coconuts for the first time. I had only ever known brown coconuts that had been imported into the UK. I learned that young coconuts are actually green and very different in texture to the brown ones with which I was familiar. Green coconuts are nutritionally almost a perfect food and naturally give you the same nutrients as electrolytes. They immediately became part of my staple diet while in India.

I also discovered that Sai Baba had a wonderful sense of humour and didn't take himself too seriously. One day, it had been raining and as Baba approached the mandir a puddle blocked his path. It was the Seva Dals' duty to ensure the pathway was clear and it was unusual for them to slip up like this. Sai Baba called the nearest Seva Dal to him. Sai Baba looked at the Seva Dal and at the puddle. The Seva Dal looked at Sai Baba and then at the puddle. Sai Baba beckoned the Seva Dal over to him and in a humorous voice said, "You don't seriously expect me to walk on water do you?" Of course those overhearing couldn't help but giggle and by lunchtime it seemed everyone in the ashram had heard about what had happened.

I had never been in such a heightened state of blissful awareness for such an extended period as I was during my time at the ashram. Synchronicity was certainly heightened to an amazing level at the ashram. It didn't make Sai Baba God though, or did it? Was he really telepathically communicating with all 30,000 people there? To listen to all the stories, it would appear so.

And what of my special request? I didn't get to see Baba's aura until the very last day and when I did it completely took me by surprise. I saw it as soon as I saw him at morning darshan. His aura was electric blue and in it was a white ring of light much like you would imagine a halo to be. I looked away and looked back but it was still there and it followed him around. I blinked. I closed my eyes for a few seconds and then reopened them but I could still see it clearly throughout the darshan. It followed him wherever he went. It was like nothing I had ever read about in books. One author's account of Baba's aura was that it was pink and stretched out to the horizon. I was happy that I wasn't projecting what I'd seen in books, as what I was seeing was nothing at all like that.

What did it mean? I reasoned that Baba could read my mind and also affect me so that I was able to see his aura, as this was not normally possible. I hadn't seen an aura so clearly before or for such a sustained period. Baba had also left it until the last day I was there to show me his aura. Had it happened sooner I would have undoubtedly had more questions to ask. It was clear then that Baba could read my mind. Although it was my last day at the ashram, Sai Baba remained as much of an enigma to me as he had been when I arrived. He felt like love, but my brain just couldn't cope with the concept of him being God, or of any human being God, though Baba continued to work with me internally after I returned to the UK.

A few years ago I started to hear some adverse publicity about Baba. The Sai Baba organisation advised devotees not to listen to or read the lies that were being told about Baba. Curiosity got the better of me, but initially I couldn't find out very much at all. Perhaps, I reasoned at the time, I wasn't meant to. It must have been about a year later that by chance I found an anti-Sai Baba website. Amongst other claims, there were accusations of child abuse and involvement in a murder. The claims about child abuse were from respectable people and as far as I could tell, seemed to be genuine. Now I was totally confused. Sai Baba had been able to talk to me in my head, to teach me lessons internally and to give me profound dreams and here he was being accused of being a possible paedophile. I knew he had helped me profoundly for which I was very grateful and yet I could not condone such behaviour as was alleged. What was I to think?

I asked for help with this and was given it within twenty-four hours. I would not like to guess whether the allegations are true or not, but this is the response I was given to help understand the accusations. Sai Baba's purpose is to help people find their own divinity, their god within. Too many people were worshipping him rather than seeing the God within themselves. What is most important to Sai Baba is that we find our god within. What we think of him is of lesser importance. To achieve his aim and help those devotees who were worshipping him to find their own divinity he has been seen to do whatever it was his devotees needed him to do to make them turn away from him and instead go within to find their god. Sai Baba continues to be an enigma to me. My brain tries to comprehend him and fails. My heart senses him and finds only love; pure love.

It is my opinion that all we need is within us and that our teacher is also within. I am very wary of giving away my power to another human being. There are though, a great many spiritual teachers on the earth plane at this time who can help show us the way. They are role models who can reflect back to us the potential that each and every one of us possesses. They can help each of us to find the god, the love and the power we all have within.

Is There Such a Thing as Fate?

I returned from India a different person; much more relaxed and at peace. I felt as though I was 'in life' but not 'of it', if that makes any sense. I watched life unfold around me, observing people's reactions but not getting caught up in any of it. I found myself not reacting in the same ways any more. The peaceful feeling lasted about two weeks and then very gradually I started being pulled back into life and into my thoughts, emotions and reactions.

My relationship with the doctor was starting to trouble me. He really didn't like me talking about what I did and had started comparing me to his schizophrenic patient whose penis sang opera to him; not the most flattering of comparisons. I knew not to try to force my views onto him and had learned to keep such matters to myself as I had no desire to make him believe what I believed. No one could have made me believe what I now believed without me having had the experiences I'd had. I'd been the biggest sceptic I knew.

The relationship was wonderful when we were together but then we would go several weeks at a time without seeing each other. I wanted to see more of him than he was prepared to give. I felt sure though, that he would come around as I had dreamt about him before meeting him and he was everything on my list. I felt sure that this one was meant to be, so when the relationship ended, I didn't really understand why. He just stopped calling me and I stopped calling him. Perhaps it was just a timing thing in that I was ready to commit to a relationship and he wasn't. In my mind I jokingly added to my list that any new partner should, 'believe in what I do, or at least be open-minded'. I realised that I could go on forever adding to my 'list' and still not get it right. I was puzzled though, as he had seemed so right on so many levels. I had come so far with learning how to access my higher guidance and yet I still wasn't getting it right.

I decided to concentrate on my spiritual practice and felt sure that I didn't want another relationship – yet. This last one hurt too much. Internally I was guided to practise meditation on a regular basis and to eat a satvic diet, which consisted basically of raw food. My healing and mediumistic abilities responded well to this new regime and I threw myself back into my work at Inner Peace and into development groups I had started to run.

In October, a rather unusual client came in for healing. Andrew was from New Zealand and explained that he had a block in his chest area that he had tried releasing through his own psychic processes, but without success. I was not used to my clients being so self-aware. The healing session itself brought another surprise. I closed my eyes and stood behind Andrew, asking for healing for him. Immediately I had to stand back. I was aware of two huge, golden columns of light, one to either side of him. They took charge of the healing, which was completed in fifteen to twenty minutes.

At the end of the healing I sat down again with Andrew. I asked him, "Do you know who your guides are?"

"Have you been talking with them?" he asked.

"No," I said. "I could just see and sense them. They took over the healing."

Andrew laughed, but didn't reveal any more. I decided to invite him to a development group I was running. "A group of us meet on a Wednesday evening to develop our abilities and talk about spiritual matters. I wondered if you would like to join us?" He said he would, but unfortunately he didn't live in the area. Then he looked at me and said, "If there is anything you want to know, I can tell you." And I felt sure he meant it.

Isn't it awful how at times like that your mind goes completely blank and you can't think of anything to ask? As we walked out of the healing room he thanked me for the healing and then introduced me to his wife and young child who had been waiting outside for him. Andrew kept in touch by phone a couple of times and invited me over to see him and his wife a couple of months later. I visited them in Loughborough. They were staying with his wife's mother and rather than stay inside and talk about subjects that would appear strange to most people we went outside for a walk.

Andrew was able to answer many of my questions. He had a very different outlook to me though. I considered myself spiritually conscious, meaning I was aware of the spiritual dimension to life. He was universally conscious and considered that universal consciousness transcended spiritual. It was a whole new concept to me. I asked Andrew's wife how she dealt with him talking like this. It was bad enough seeing dead people and trying to get others to understand what that was like, but this concept of universal consciousness blew my mind. I knew I was hard to live with, but this must be even harder. "I am used to it now," his wife said.

I didn't see or hear from Andrew again until January when I got a call. He said, "I'm just phoning to say goodbye and wondering if you would like to meet up one last time before I head back to New Zealand?"

"You are going back?" I asked, surprised by the news.

"Yes," he said. "I am about to book my flight. I can't stay here any longer. It is too tense with my ex-wife and her family."

"You are going back alone?" I asked.

"Yes," he confirmed. "My wife and I legally separated at the beginning of last year. She lives over here now and I live in New Zealand. I just came over to see our son."

I hadn't realised that they were separated. I had taken them to be a family. Our discussions had always focused on spiritual rather than personal matters. And sometimes although I am psychic, I can miss what is blindingly obvious.

Andrew and I agreed to meet and he came over the following weekend. We had lots to talk about. He stayed into the evening and as he sat in the armchair to my side I saw he had with him a young girl of five or six. She was beautiful with long, blonde hair and blue eyes. I didn't mention that I had seen her until much later. I wondered who she was and why she was with him. It would take me a while to find out. Andrew and

I had a lot in common, although we disagreed a lot too. I wasn't looking for a relationship, concentrating as I was on my spiritual practice and in any case at eight years my junior he was too young for me. It took me by surprise then, when we started to have feelings towards one another.

The relationship developed and Andrew decided not to return to New Zealand. Very soon, he moved in with me and started helping out at Inner Peace. Meditation was now part of my daily practice and as I meditated one morning I found that I could not relax part of my stomach. Instead it tingled. I moved my consciousness into the tingling. It tingled even more. I wondered what it meant and internally asked if I was pregnant. "Would you like to be?" came the response. This was high-level guidance. I had learnt by then that the higher-level guidance rarely gives advice but instead asks you questions to help you clarify your choices.

I thought about the whole issue of pregnancy. My relationship with Andrew was very new and I knew I had to decide if I wanted this baby, even if there wasn't going to be a father around to help me bring him or her up. I weighed up all the pros and cons and decided I did want this baby. As soon as I had made my choice, the response came, "Yes you are pregnant." Before telling anyone in my family, being practical as always, I decided to do a pregnancy test. I bought the test and

Andrew waited outside the bathroom to hear the news. Sure enough, I was pregnant, but we had both known internally that it would be positive. We had only known each other such a short space of time that we wondered what we would do.

Was the universe delivering me my greatest fear; being a single mother? Or was this meant to be? Was Andrew the one for me? Was the universe giving me the strongest possible sign that we should be together? I had not been looking for a relationship and I certainly wasn't looking to have a baby. When I fell pregnant so soon into the relationship with Andrew I questioned why and in particular why it didn't happen in the previous relationship. I didn't know whether the relationship with Andrew was right for me or whether I was supposed to bring up this child by myself. There were so many unknowns. I wanted to do the right thing for all of us, but not having this child never entered my head.

I looked at the situation from all possible angles. I realised that I had carried an internal fear of being a solo mum right the way through from adolescence. Perhaps I had to face my fear? I realised that by bringing the fear of being a solo mum into consciousness and releasing it I would not have to go through the experience in physical reality and nor would my child, so I made that my priority.

From a really practical point of view, children are made from their mother and father's genes. There is an innate bond between them regardless of the love that each is able to show the other. Both Andrew's and my own previous relationships had finished and each of us still had emotional baggage to work through, but we were both available to commit to each other and to this new baby. Andrew and I were both adult and though we might not have the feelings towards each other to make the relationship last long term, we could at least give it our best shot and see what developed.

And that is what we did. Each of us had different insights along the way. We grew from liking one another to truly loving one another and we each went through huge personal growth along the way. We challenged one another, inspired, annoyed and cared for one another and it was worth it. We found ourselves through our relationship and our relationship continues to grow as we grow. We put a lot into it and we get a lot back.

Now, some years on, I realise that relationships are all about our relationship with ourselves. The relationships we find ourselves in are like mirrors that reflect back to us how we feel about ourselves. When, in a much earlier relationship, I didn't trust myself and my own feelings, I attracted a partner I couldn't trust. My gut would tell me he was being unfaithful again.

He would deny it, at least initially, and we would go round in circles until one day I decided to trust my feelings. The relationship ended and my next partner didn't sleep around. I knew then I had learned a lesson and would not have to suffer an unfaithful partner unless I chose to. When I was worried what people thought of me I attracted to me a partner who didn't believe in what I did; the doctor. He had been absolutely right for me at that time.

I have seen many people over the years who have complained about their partner not understanding them. Often the real problem is that they do not understand themselves and once they work on this, suddenly their partner does understand them, or they attract to themselves a new partner who is understanding. Similarly, I have seen many people who wish their partner could be more loving, romantic and sensual. By turning it around to how they could become more of these things themselves, the whole situation transforms.

The best advice I have ever received about relationships came while I was washing the dishes one day. I was running Andrew down in my head. Why didn't he help more? Couldn't he see how busy I was? He never helped with the dishes and so on. I was heavily pregnant at the time and felt my grievances were justified. "Just be kind to each other," popped into my head. Andrew came in and rather than being moody about all I had to do I was kind to him. He came to talk and dried the dishes while I washed. It was the first time he had helped with the dishes in months! Our relationship never looked back. I learned that moaning or whinging about a relationship didn't solve anything. It just kept you in that same situation. By moaning you were effectively giving away your power in the situation.

I learned that moaning to girlfriends had the same effect too. How often as a woman had I contributed to conversations where a group of women ran down the men in their lives? The same conversations would be played out week after week. What a waste of time and energy. I was grateful at last to be conscious of what I had been doing and to have the opportunity to do things differently. Being kind made perfect sense and sat well with me. It is easy to just ask yourself every now and then, "Am I being kind to this other person?" whoever they may be. Being kind doesn't take any more time, but it does change your whole state of being. I can wholeheartedly recommend it!

Becoming pregnant raised the issue of whether such things are fate or destiny and unable to be avoided. Clearly the child I was expecting was not an immaculate conception. It was more an immaculate lack of contraception. If we had made different choices the baby would not be here. So our free will had some part to play, but to what extent? I reflected over my life to date, considering to what extent any of it was fated or destined, to what extent it was all my free will choice. Was seeing spirits and tapping into healing abilities my destiny or did I create it?

From my experience of clairvoyance – clear seeing into the past, present and future – I knew that people created their own realities because if I did a reading for someone and they didn't like what they heard they had the free will to change it. It wasn't physically possible for me to see the same things twice for a person. The very act of giving them a reading brought into their consciousness how they were creating their future in the present moment and that knowledge in itself empowered them to create a new improved future for themselves. So if I did a reading and then did a second reading straight afterwards the second would be noticeably different to the first.

I could never have imagined some of the things that have happened to me in my life yet some of the things I had been told by clairvoyants years earlier, and many of the things I had clairvoyantly told others had come true. One lady in particular sprang to mind. When I first took her call I thought, because of the way she began the story that she was phoning to complain. She had seen me six months ago and I had told her that her husband would be back in six months. On Friday night she had been sitting in her lounge reflecting that it was six months to the day that her husband had left and he wasn't back. She was not happy about the fact nor about the fifteen pounds she felt she had wasted on my reading. Suddenly there was a tap on the window. She pulled back the curtains to see her husband there, with his suitcase.

How did that happen? Did I see the future or did I plant the seed so strongly within that lady that she made it come true? I couldn't work it out in my own mind so it was time to go beyond my own limited thinking. I asked on a percentage basis to what extent our thoughts and beliefs create our experience of reality and to what extent does our experience of reality create our thoughts and beliefs? A long silence followed and so I got on with other menial tasks while the answer came back. It arrived. "In one hundred percent of cases our thoughts create our experience of reality." It was explained further. "If you believe that your experience of reality creates your thoughts, that is based on a belief, therefore all your experiences of reality are based on your thoughts and beliefs." Logically it made sense I supposed, but it was hard to initially grasp the idea that our thoughts are the source of what we create here.

The concept conveyed at the same time was that there is what I can best describe as a field of consciousness of which we are all part. Because of the interconnectedness of all things, all that we hold within us as thoughts or beliefs automatically manifest in the life we experience around us. Some of our experiences are caused by a belief held by the mass consciousness and some experiences are caused by a belief held by individual consciousness. Our physical law of cause and effect evidences this. Cause and effect would not be possible without the interconnectedness of all things. I remembered an earlier teaching along these lines that was now being explained even more fully.

We are not yet conscious of some beliefs that we hold and this is why we have created the concept of time passing in a linear fashion. Time allows us to experience our thoughts and beliefs in a linear fashion, rather than all at once so that we can learn how a particular belief held individually or collectively affects our life. Here on earth we get to learn about ourselves as creators. In other dimensions or forms, we learn different lessons and time as we know it here is not necessary.

When we experience something in our life, we get to choose how we respond. We can respond in a reactive way, our unconscious programming triggering feelings and emotions within us, or we can respond consciously, looking at how we may have contributed to the situation at some level and what we now choose to do about it.

The question for me now was what did I choose to create in my life?

A Family

At seven months pregnant I awoke one morning to find the bed wet. It was my first pregnancy and I wasn't sure what was happening to me as I hadn't yet attended antenatal classes. I presumed that the baby must have caused me to wet the bed. I mentioned it to my mum and she was not quite so calm. She was concerned that my waters may have broken. I assured her that there wasn't that much water and that I felt sure I must have just had a weak bladder. Mum insisted that I phone my midwife and wouldn't leave until I made the call.

I called my midwife who directed Andrew and I to go straight to Chesterfield Hospital, a twenty minute drive away. At the hospital no one seemed at all concerned about what was happening to me and it was over three hours before I was seen. The view seemed to be that if my waters had broken I would know about it. We very nearly turned around and went home.

Everything changed though, once I had been examined. My waters had indeed broken and I was admitted immediately. They asked how far into the pregnancy I was and I told them that I was thirty-one weeks. They asked whether I knew if I was expecting a boy or a girl. I didn't realise at the time why that was important. A wheelchair was summoned for me and I was told that I would have to lie down as much as possible now and only get up to go to the toilet. The baby's heartbeat was checked and a scan was arranged for early that afternoon. The scan confirmed that the baby was fine and that there was still sufficient amniotic fluid for the moment.

I was temporarily admitted to a ward and some of the other pregnant mums came over to see me. I didn't even look pregnant to them. They couldn't wait to have their babies and here I was trying to hold mine back. Andrew was sent home to get an overnight bag for me and I was left in the ward with my feelings. I didn't know what was happening to me or what it meant to have your waters break. I assumed I would just rest for the last two months of the pregnancy and I wasn't unduly concerned.

What I didn't know at the time was that Andrew had had a reading done by a clairvoyant he respected and she had told him that the baby I was carrying would not go full term, implying that it would not survive.

He was going through hell and didn't want to leave my side, but he bravely kept his fears to himself.

A few hours passed and eventually a doctor came to see me. He explained that now my waters had broken there was a risk of infection and so the baby would only be able to survive within the womb for a week at the very most. The aim would be to stop me from going into labour for as long as possible while checking my temperature hourly. If there were any signs of an infection then they would induce labour.

I didn't understand how well my baby would be developed at thirty-one weeks. The doctor explained that there were likely to be some physical problems, perhaps with breathing, as the lungs would not have fully developed but that they would administer steroids to minimise the risk of this. I took whatever they offered. I wasn't aware at that time of the risks of steroids and the doctor spoke of it so routinely as though there wasn't a choice. At thirty-one weeks the chances of survival were good but could not be guaranteed. They told me that the chances would be better if I was carrying a girl, as girls tend to be fighters. I deliberately hadn't asked to be told the sex of my baby at the initial scan but felt it was a girl. I already had the name Sarah for her, after my late grandmother, my best friend and a young girl I had been very close to.

The bad news was that I couldn't stay at the hospital. After all they had just told me I was amazed that they couldn't let me stay there. It was explained that there were not sufficient incubators and so they would move me to another hospital. Sheffield Hospital was their first choice, but from my viewpoint that was at least an hour's drive from home and would make visiting difficult for Andrew and my mum. Andrew returned with my hospital bag and did not take the news about changing hospitals at all well though I still didn't know why he was so anxious. A nurse reported that Sheffield could not take me either so they would be trying further afield at York, Leeds and the other main Sheffield hospital. An hour later we received the disappointing news that all were full.

At quarter to nine at night a place was eventually found for me at Nottingham Hospital. The journey by ambulance took about an hour and a half. They had to travel extra slowly so as not to induce labour. Andrew had to follow in his car, as he was not allowed to travel with me, which I found incredible. It was just after midnight when I finally arrived at Nottingham Hospital. It had been a very long, emotionally draining day and I could not believe it when they wanted another male doctor to give me an internal examination before they would admit me. Everyone had been telling me how important it was not to bring labour on, so I was terrified of having another internal examination and refused. It was after midnight for heaven's sake! I must have made my point as they took me straight into the ward.

I managed to keep labour at bay for five days. The nurses would remind me to let them know if I felt any contractions and I would invariably ask, "What is a contraction?" Again, because I hadn't attended antenatal classes, I had no idea what to expect which with hindsight turned out to be just as well. They couldn't really describe contractions to me, as they said labour was different for everyone, which did nothing to reassure me.

One evening I was getting what felt like a period pain. It was 9:00 pm and visiting time was ending. I asked Andrew to stay while the stomach pain went, as if it did turn out to be a contraction he would have a two hour round trip to get back to the hospital. The nurses were really helpful and accommodating. I asked one of the nurses again if what I was experiencing could be contractions but they didn't really seem strong enough. By 11:00 pm, however, it was clear that something was definitely going on. It was more than a period pain. I also had a man with me in spirit form who told me that everything would be alright and I absolutely believed him. He said that he would be with me all the way through the birth and explained that the contractions were simply a natural way of warming up the muscles ready for the birth itself. I should not resist them, as that would make them painful; just go with them, relax into them and breathe with them.

The contractions steadily increased until at midnight I was moved into the labour room. A midwife eventually came to see me and said I would be having a Caesarean section and that she was just waiting on the doctor who was delivering triplets. "No I am not." I answered back between contractions. "I am having a natural birth."

"No, you are having a Caesar," she replied equally abruptly. "The baby is not sufficiently advanced to have a natural birth," and with that she left the room. There was no way I was having a Caesar. I knew I was in labour now and I was too far along. The midwife returned to check on me ten minutes later and sure enough she found I was nine centimetres dilated. "You only have another centimetre to go. It looks as though you will be having a natural birth after all," she said.

At ten minutes past two on the morning of the 10th of October 1998 Sarah Amaris was born weighing three pounds, fourteen and a half ounces. You know babies are small when they give you their weight in half ounces. The birth had taken a matter of hours. The midwife was excellent and let me hold Sarah briefly before she had to go to be checked. She was beautiful.

Early signs were that our daughter was okay, though a bit on the small side. I had known it but it was still good to hear.

Because of her small size, Sarah needed to be kept in an incubator to help keep her warm and to be fed via a tube until she developed the sucking reflex which usually develops somewhere between thirty-two and thirty-four weeks. It was hard seeing our newborn child in an incubator and not being able to touch or cuddle her. Small cuddles were allowed but I wanted to cuddle her all the time. I had to learn to express milk so that when the time came I would be able to feed Sarah myself.

The night I was in labour, a young girl expecting triplets had also come in by ambulance. She was in a labour room at the same time as me but was quite rightly given priority as her three babies together weighed less than Sarah. The smallest weighed just one pound. Like me, her local hospital did not have enough incubators and she had travelled even further, from Middlesbrough I think. She had been transported at a very slow speed along the motorway while extreme measures had been taken to stop her giving birth. All this at eighteen or nineteen years of age! My experience had been nothing compared to hers and even now she did not know if her babies, three boys, were going to live or have physical problems now or in the future. I wondered how she and her young partner would cope and my heart went out to them. It put our own situation into perspective.

We were very fortunate. Sarah could breathe by herself and the incubator was only necessary to help her retain her body temperature. I was expressing breast milk and she was feeding well. Nothing prepared us then, for walking into the special care unit one morning and finding Sarah in the middle of an operation in front of everyone in the open unit, with blood everywhere. A long line lead was being put into her as she was rejecting her food. We had been neither consulted nor warned that we would walk into seeing this.

Overnight the nurses had increased Sarah's feed as she was doing so well and as a result had run out of my breast milk. They had decided to give her formula rather than asking me to express some more milk, which I would willingly have done. They didn't know that milk allergies run in both Andrew's and my families. We felt sure that once back on breast milk she would stop rejecting the milk and she did. We were angry about how the whole situation was handled and at not being consulted but we didn't complain as all of the staff had hearts of gold and were doing their very best. We knew that!

Sarah continued to improve and soon learned to breastfeed. We were transferred back to Chesterfield Hospital for a couple of weeks, as that was much closer to home and once Sarah was increasing her body weight we were eventually free to go home. It was what we had wanted for so long. On my last night in hospital I sat on my hospital bed holding Sarah and looking at her and I cried. At just five pounds Andrew could cup her head in his hand and her feet would just touch the inside of his elbow. She was still so very small and it was such a huge responsibility I wondered how I would cope.

Sarah Amaris was a very good baby and my fears of coping with her at home soon faded. I had called her Sarah after significant people in my life and Andrew, wanting to add something more original, came up with the name Amaris. Months after her birth we found out that her name had a very special meaning. Sarah means princess in Hebrew and Amar means love in Latin. By adding 'is' on the end to make Amaris we had changed the meaning to 'of love'. Sarah was our princess of love. We couldn't have found a more fitting name if we had tried.

Sarah was so small that regular babies clothes would not fit her. Everything had to be made or borrowed from the special care baby unit. Visitors had to be kept to a minimum for the first month to prevent the risk of infection. It was heartwarming to receive so many gifts, flowers and letters from well-wishers and it was good to be home.

We had been at home for about a month when quite a large lump suddenly appeared on Sarah's stomach. Our midwife referred us to the doctor and the doctor referred us to a specialist at Sheffield Children's Hospital later that same day. We knew it was not a good sign for the referral to be made so quickly. Sarah needed a double hernia operation and was booked in for the following day. I went to pieces. There was no reassurance this time in my head. No one was with me. I knew in my head, logically, that the situation was nowhere near as bad as her premature birth could have been. It was an operation with minimal risk that they performed every day, but Sarah was still so small at less than six pounds and was still weeks from the date on which she would have been born had she gone full term.

I realised just what other people went through when they didn't have access to the inner knowing that I usually had. I was being taught compassion. It is not a lesson I would care to repeat. Thankfully, Sarah's operation went well; she was allowed home with us the next day and went from strength to strength. Her prematurity did not seem to be affecting her in any way. I realised for the first time that she was the girl I had seen at Andrew's side that first time he had come to visit me and that I had seen her spirit form waiting to come through into physical form. I wondered if

Andrew and I were supposed to have got together earlier than we did. Perhaps then she would not have needed to be premature.

Motherhood was difficult for me. I loved Sarah with all my heart but had been used to working all my life and had not really valued the role of mother. The society I grew up in promoted and recognised achievement and I could not easily feel achievement in changing nappies and doing housework. It was hard for me to adjust to. I was also used to being the main breadwinner while now I would receive just two hundred pounds a month for six months, the standard maternity pay, before I had to start earning again. If you are self-employed in the UK, you can't just stop working and go on a benefit. The whole business would have had to close, meaning Mum would have had to stop working too. Effectively I would have had to become bankrupt before I could get any further assistance. Had I still been working for the bank I would have got six months paid leave and could then have returned to part time work. I kicked myself once again. Why did I leave? But I soon came to realise that if I had not left the bank I would not have met Andrew and if I had not met Andrew, Sarah would not be here. The message was that I needed to deal with the situation facing me now rather than what might have been.

I had never claimed a benefit in my life as I had never needed to and now that I needed to, I couldn't. Financially then, being a full time mum wasn't an option and yet I was not prepared to leave my baby with a stranger so I could go to work. For a few months, Mum, Andrew and I tried managing the shop and Sarah between us. Initially it worked quite well because Sarah was such a good baby and slept for much of the time, but it wasn't a long-term solution.

When Sarah was about eight months old, Andrew got a call to say his mum in New Zealand wasn't well. He didn't want to leave Sarah and me but we couldn't afford flights for all of us, so he went on his own. While he was away, I had a dream. I was standing at the side of a motorway talking to his younger sister. She asked me how I felt about just leaving everything and going over to New Zealand. I said I was fine with it and inside I felt that way too. I told Andrew about it on the phone that night but didn't really understand its significance for two more days. Then, on bank holiday Monday I was travelling north on the A1, a dual carriageway, with four children, including Sarah in my car. A new driver in his first attempt at driving on a motorway, rather than using the slip road, pulled out of a service station straight in front of me. Can you believe that in the UK you can pass your driving test without ever driving on a motorway? I saw him pull out but couldn't believe what I was seeing. There was only one other lane and because it was bank holiday there was heavy traffic. I braked as hard as I could but I had nowhere to go. The car spun and spun. Someone screamed; I think it was me. Bang! We stopped as the car hit the median barrier. I was amazed that I had not hit anything else.

I got out of the car, fully expecting to leave my physical body behind, to be dead. Amazingly I wasn't and nor was anyone else. Apart from whiplash, no one was even injured though the car was a write-off. The accident shook us all up and when Andrew heard he was very upset and wanted to fly straight back to us. I asked for some guidance about why the accident had happened and was told that it was time for my life to take a different direction. Symbolically, my vehicle had come to rest pointing in another direction. This was the beginning of my realisation that I did want to be a full-time mum and that if I couldn't do it in the UK, perhaps I would be able to in New Zealand. When I told Andrew he wasn't at all sure about my plans. He suggested that perhaps I should take more time to think it over. Andrew's first wife hadn't liked living in New Zealand and had never really settled so had come back to the UK with their son, so he was concerned that I might sell everything up and then not like it as well.

That evening as I lay in bed I remembered my dream a few days earlier; the motorway, Andrew's sister and going to New Zealand. Was the dream referring to this new direction in my life? My decision was galvanised a few days later when my insurance company rang about my claim for my car. The car had been written off as I had expected and they wanted to offer me a sum in payment. The man on the phone offered me several hundred pounds more than the 'book value' of the car. I was shocked and didn't respond. The person on the other end of the phone took my silence as a refusal and promptly increased the offer further. I accepted and the cheque was banked within the week. Have you ever known an insurance company to settle so quickly?

I booked Sarah and myself on a flight to New Zealand and left myself just two weeks to sell everything up. I decided to have a garage sale and placed adverts in the local papers. I prepared a flyer listing all the main items I had for sale, and decided that I would post it through the letterboxes of neighbours before the sale.

Time was flying by and there was so much to do that on the Friday before the weekend of the garage sale I still hadn't got the flyers posted, so I got up early with Sarah, put her in a front carrier and started putting the flyers in neighbours' letterboxes. I was about halfway through when my bus to Inner Peace arrived. It normally didn't arrive early yet here it was ten minutes before time. I was cross that it had to be early today of all days as now I would never get to post the rest of the flyers, but I had to catch it. Without a car, there was no other way of getting to work that day and particularly not when I was carrying Sarah.

I arrived at work ten minutes early and so had time to call in at my bank. I still had the flyers for the garage sale in my hand, so passed one over to the teller to put on the staff notice board. That teller came to the garage sale and bought more than half the household items I was selling! The universe was intervening once again and presumably assisting in my move to New Zealand.

With just a few days to go before Sarah and I would be boarding a plane to join Andrew, I was starting to struggle with the thought of leaving my family behind and especially Mum. Having taken such an active role looking after Sarah, Mum was so close to her and she was very close to me too. We had worked together and lived together over the past few years. But I knew I had to go to New Zealand. I knew it was a dream and perhaps it was a pipe dream, but perhaps Andrew and I really could make it a reality.

A New Home

It was harder than I ever imagined saying goodbye to Mum at Heathrow Airport. I knew that she would always be there for me if things didn't work out with Andrew in New Zealand, but neither of us knew how long it would be before we saw each other or she saw her much-loved granddaughter Sarah again. My flight was called and we said a tearful farewell. Sarah and I were on our way. It was only four weeks since we had waved Andrew off at the same airport to see his ill mother, and now it was our turn.

The airline personnel were excellent. They couldn't do enough for me. I would occasionally get a pitying look from one of the other passengers; a mother alone with a child, trying to carry a nine month old and luggage, but I knew it was not for long and that Andrew would be waiting for me. I wondered how solo mums managed. I could so easily have walked that path if I had made a different choice. Waiting in the departure lounge to board the flight, I sat next to a really nice lady called Barbara who, like me, was heading to New Zealand and in fact to New Plymouth, which was the exact same city as me.

I had a special seat on the plane, just in front of the television screens. There was space there to put a bassinet when Sarah wanted to sleep. The problem was, Sarah had never slept in a bassinet. She always slept in bed with Andrew and me and I wasn't sure that she would settle in a bassinet. It felt awfully hard and uncomfortable. A middle-aged man was taking his place diagonally across from me and he looked daggers in my direction. "That baby had better be quiet," he growled. I could hardly believe my ears, but found myself saying, "Yes, she's a very good baby." I prayed that she would be. A friend had warned me that babies could be disturbed by the change in altitude so it was a good idea to feed them on take off and landing to help their ears. I was glad I was still breastfeeding Sarah. It made for a quiet flight from the man's viewpoint at least.

I was thrilled when I saw that Barbara, the friendly lady from the boarding gate was sitting next to me on the plane. What a happy coincidence it seemed to be as she was good company and I think she felt the same way too. As we talked, she told me that her husband had passed away and I knew then that our sitting together was no coincidence; we had been put together for a reason. It is funny but ever since my spiritual awakening, whenever I have travelled by plane I have always sat next to someone who has recently been bereaved. I do not always tell them that I am a medium as that may not fit everyone's beliefs but somehow the right things seem to come out of my mouth. I know the right thing to say to help them and I feel they become more peaceful. Sometimes all I need to do is listen. People need to talk about their loved ones who have passed over. This is something we can all do for one another.

The first flight was about twelve or thirteen hours. I tried putting Sarah in the bassinet a couple of times but only succeeded in waking her up. Instead, I held her in my arms, not daring to let myself sleep in case I dropped her. It passed quite quickly, but my arms ached from holding her. When the plane eventually landed I even got a smile out of the middle-aged gentleman when he left. "You were right! She has been a very good baby," he said. I suspected his initial harsh words to me had preyed on his mind during the flight. He had probably just been tired and wanting to sleep.

The stewardesses said they would try to get me three seats together for the next flight of over eleven hours so I could lie down with Sarah and get some sleep. It was a nice thought but it would be a different plane with a different crew and I didn't hold out much hope that they would be able to arrange it for me. Boarding the second flight there were some spare seats but not three together. After take off, however, a stewardess came to see me. They had asked a gentleman who had three seats to himself to change places with me and he had agreed. What a wonderful man. I never got the chance to thank him but was extremely grateful for the chance to stretch out and sleep.

The second flight passed much more quickly than the first and soon we were getting ready to land. Walking off the plane I could feel how much warmer the weather was in Auckland. It was the beginning of June. I had left an English summer and gone into a New Zealand winter and it was warmer! Andrew was waiting for Sarah and me and it was a moving reunion. I felt like I was home and that I could at last relax. I slept for most of the car journey back to New Plymouth.

It was good to see Andrew again. It had been difficult for both of us, being apart and Andrew couldn't believe how much Sarah had changed in the month since he had last seen her. We stayed with Andrew's parents initially until we decided what we wanted to do. Within two weeks there was another happy coincidence. A tenant of Andrew's parents needed to give notice on a house he was renting from them. He asked whether he could leave sooner than the usual month's notice period. We were thrilled. In just a couple of weeks we would have our own house. It was small but it would be ours. The house was sunny and light with a large garden for Sarah to play in when she was older. Andrew's family was great, helping us get together all we needed for our new home and then helping us to move in.

I had been guided to New Zealand so that I could be a full-time Mum, so I put all my energies into making the most of motherhood, finding new friends, going to play group and adjusting to my new life. My involvement in mediumship and healing took a back seat.

I hadn't been in New Zealand long, just a few weeks in fact, when I discovered I was pregnant again. The pregnancy felt different this time and I felt sure that this time it would be a boy. I was under the care of a paediatrician because Sarah was premature, but the pregnancy was quite straightforward until I reached seven months when premature contractions started. This time, I knew what they felt like and I was admitted to hospital and given an injection to stop the labour but I was told it would only be given once. It was to give time for me to have a series of steroid injections to help the baby's lungs develop. The injection to stop the contractions worked and I went home again.

A few days passed before the contractions started once more and I was readmitted to hospital. The contractions were coming frequently and strongly and the nurses suggested I take a warm bath to relax, which I did and the contractions stopped once more. We were all surprised but very glad as the baby still had weeks to go before full term. They kept me overnight at the hospital and then discharged me again. Because the baby's head was engaged, and had been for at least a week, I went backwards and forwards like this to hospital over the next several days. No one really knew what was going on as contractions would start and then stop again. I had another scan and it revealed I was about a month further on than the doctors had initially thought, which was such a relief.

When Liam James finally came into the world at 8:30 at night on 30th March 2000 he was just two weeks premature. His head was very bruised from being engaged for such a long time but apart from that he was fine. We were both discharged from hospital after twenty-four hours and a midwife arranged to call in to see us in our home the next morning. I thought everything was fine, but on her first visit the midwife was clearly worried about Liam's colour as she thought he looked a bit jaundiced. I could see what she meant. The midwife asked if he had any unusual sores or blisters anywhere on his body and I told her that I had not seen any. She said that it was just a precaution and that she was just checking. She said that Liam would have to go back in to see a paediatrician and that he would probably just need ultraviolet light treatment to help the jaundice. When Sarah was first born she too needed some UV light treatment and so we weren't too concerned about it as we knew what was involved.

We returned to the hospital later that day and were surprised to find Liam had to go into the Special Baby Unit, the equivalent of the Special Care Unit in the UK. We were already familiar with all the scrubbing up procedures from having Sarah in a similar unit and settled easily into the routines. A few hours of light treatment turned into days and then into two weeks. We asked why and it seemed that the bruising to his head was worse than they had at first thought and the blood was taking some processing by his liver. Liam needed a lot of ultraviolet light to stay on top of it.

Again someone else's situation put our own situation into perspective. A young couple had lost one twin and the other was in the unit, fighting for his life. He had a staphylococcal infection and had lost most of his skin through it. The doctors were struggling to get the infection under control. I couldn't even look at the baby in the incubator. Just the thought of a baby without skin was too much for me to bear. I found it hard to imagine what the baby's parents were going through being unable to hold their only surviving child.

At last Liam was given the all clear to go home. I find hospitals draining, so it had been hard staying in the hospital on my own with Liam, even though Andrew and Sarah came to see us at every opportunity. It seemed like we had lived on hospital food for weeks.

Changing Liam next morning I noticed there was a little blister on his chest and then another on his back. I phoned the midwife, who came around as soon as she could. Liam was admitted back into the Special Baby Unit that day but this time into the isolation unit. The baby without any skin was in the main part of the SBU and Liam was in the isolation ward. What did it mean? After about an hour of waiting we were told that Liam had a staphylococcal infection like the other baby.

Plan A was to give a large dose of antibiotics intravenously and hope that they worked. Plan B . . . ? There was no plan B. We were warned that there was a chance Liam would die. Medical science didn't have a solution for this infection. I remembered hearing about a horrific flesh-eating bacterial infection in the UK that was sweeping through hospitals. It had sounded so far-fetched, yet now, for us, it was a reality. We were told that it would be twenty-four hours before we knew if the antibiotics had worked. I don't think anyone in the family in New Zealand or in the UK slept that night and yet Liam looked so healthy that it was hard to accept that he was extremely ill.

We were overwhelmed by the fear of losing our son. We prayed harder than we had ever done in our lives and sent Liam healing almost constantly. It was the longest twenty-four hours of our lives. Eventually the test results came back. The antibiotics had worked. Both Andrew and I were numb and it took a while for the good news to sink in. They told me that I would have to stay in the unit with Liam until all the sores healed and then we would be able to go home. The sores started to heal and each time I changed Liam, his skin appeared to be getting better and better. I breathed a sigh of relief each time I changed him and found no new sores. It meant we were that much closer to going home. Another week or so passed before we went home but this time, we went home for good and there were no further problems with Liam.

We had just settled into a routine of our own when the share-milker on Andrew's parents' farm in Hawera walked off the property at a time when another share-milker could not easily be engaged. The share-milker's wife had lost a much-wanted baby and our hearts went out to them both as we had come so close to losing our son too. It seemed a logical solution for Andrew to go to Hawera to run the family farm.

Andrew started on the farm immediately and Sarah, Liam and I were to follow at the end of the week. There was a lot to do and no time to dwell on what we had just been through, which was perhaps just as well. The farmhouse had five bedrooms and a swimming pool.

Though it needed a coat of paint, I had always enjoyed decorating so I was quite looking forward to it and we would have so much more space and a fantastic view of Mount Taranaki. But farm life was not at all as I imagined.

On a farm this size, it was normal that both the husband and wife helped with milking the cows. I hadn't realised how much of a 'townie' I was. I was not used to living on a farm and I worried that I would not be able to cope. I found it particularly hard looking after Sarah who was now nineteen months old and Liam who was now six weeks old and now I was expected to milk cows as well. I had no idea how other farming mums managed. Thankfully, my mother-in-law Mary came to our aid and was an absolute Godsend. You couldn't wish for a better mother-in-law. She knew just how to help in a way that wasn't interfering and I was able to spend most of my time with the children, occasionally helping with a milking to give her a break.

I had much to learn about farming, starting with the very obvious things, such as shutting gates after me, to the not so obvious. For example I had never realised previously that cows had to have a calf to produce milk. I knew they had four stomachs and I had just assumed that they ate grass and turned it into milk. I was in for a rude awakening. Each year cows have to produce a calf to start their milk producing and if they don't calve in time to suit the farmer, healthy calves are simply aborted. On our farm of two hundred and twenty cows, between thirty and forty would usually be aborted. This would not happen if Andrew and I had anything to do with it. We cajoled, coerced and guilt-tripped the rest of the family into not aborting calves the year we were there. I even threatened to walk off the farm with the children if it happened and I would have done.

Just because something has been done in the past doesn't mean it is right. Humanity is being called to wake up and in doing so we must wake up to what we are doing and see it with fresh eyes. Though many people are not, I was in a position where I could influence events and I feel that if we can see what needs to be done, we must do it to the best of our ability. The local vet said we were the only farm she knew of in Taranaki, a huge area, that wasn't aborting.

Another distressing reality of farm life, is that the calves that are born naturally are almost immediately taken from their mothers. This was distressing for me to observe let alone to witness the ongoing distress of the animals. Cows would at times take down fence after fence to get to their calves. One even killed herself in her desperation. Some farmers will tell you it has to be that way but to me it was insane to take the calves from their mothers and then handfeed them either colostrum from the herd or reconstituted milk made from milk powder. It was no wonder that calves would occasionally get sick.

Any sickly calves went to the bobby pen outside the farm gate to be picked up and taken to the abattoir. Not from our farm that year they didn't. I saw bobby calves taken from other farms being literally thrown into the back of a truck onto other living animals. In my head I was reminded of a quote from Gandhi when on one occasion he was asked what he thought about western civilisation. He said he thought it would be a good idea. Now I knew what he meant.

I had no idea that all this happened on dairy farms and I had always taken the availability of milk very much for granted. I did once ask my higher guidance what we needed to do to put things right with milking and the impression I received was that we shouldn't be doing it at all. Cows' milk is designed for calves, not humans, and that is why it causes so many health problems in people. It will, however, be many years before significant changes are made. We humans like our milk, ice-cream and cheese. Many of us choose to put our taste buds before both our health and our conscience.

We had tried to do right by the cows as best we could but I was glad when our time share-milking came to an end. We used homeopathy rather than antibiotics and tried to look after the earth by doing things organically but it was a small drop in a very big ocean and we knew that in all likelihood, the next year it would all be back to how it was before with a new share-milker and calves being aborted. I understood that I could not change everything. Some things are going to take many years to change, perhaps generations, but that is no excuse not to do your very best. Often the little acts we consider to be too small to make a difference, ripple out and somehow, some way prick someone else's conscience. We remind them of what they do already know and we make a difference. One day I hope Andrew and I will go back and finish what we started, transforming the family farm to an organic farm where calves are reared with their mothers and there is full consideration for the interconnectedness of all things.

After share-milking for about six months we returned to our small house in New Plymouth. Soon after that we all took a trip back to the UK to tie up the loose ends of the business and to visit family. It was great to renew our links with family and the healing centre and I found that it rekindled my desire to become psychically active again, so on our return to New Zealand I visited the local New Age crystal shop. I was amazed to find it was called Inner Piece. I reasoned that this must be the right place for me as it had the same name as my own shop in the UK, only spelled differently. Their spelling was deliberately chosen as their main activity was selling crystals, which they felt were an inner piece of the earth. I enquired if they needed any clairvoyant readers and they did. I met the owner and got on very well with him so I started the following week.

It was great to be doing readings again and I was pleasantly surprised to find that my abilities were still sharp. Word soon got around and I had a steady stream of customers including many professional people. The demand was mainly for clairvoyance, people wanting to know what the future had in store for them, but occasionally I would get a request for mediumship. Increasingly I started to recognise the need for workshops and I started a business running classes in meditation, psychic development and healing.

Many people wanted to know how to do what I did and I was happy to share with them what I knew. My experience as a trainer stood me in good stead. I reflected on how well the universe had prepared me for where I now was and what I was doing. Little did my boss at Lloyds Bank know all those years ago when he sent me on that expensive course that this was how I would be using those advanced skills. I had always envisaged having my own training company, helping people be all that they could be, but I had never dreamed that I would be teaching people such amazing things and affecting them so profoundly.

At home Sarah and Liam were growing quickly and our little house was starting to feel cramped. I felt that it would be nice to move somewhere with a bit more space so I decided to ask the universe to help and wrote myself a note; "I intend to have a three-bedroomed house in the country for $150,000 or less, provided it is for my highest good, harming no one and for the good of all."

Within three days Andrew and I had found a house but the vendor wouldn't budge on the price she wanted which was $153,500. Moreover, the vendor wasn't prepared to move out for three months. I couldn't understand it. My intent had been very clear and I had even written my request down, but the mystery was soon explained. By the weekend, Andrew had found another house he preferred. I visited it and liked it too, so we ended up purchasing it, our dream home, which was much more suitable than the first house and just what we needed at that time, for under $150,000.

Increasingly, I realised that my experiences were teaching me to become more conscious of the choices I was making. I was encouraged to play a more active role in creating my life and aligning my life choices with who I really was. I was shown that life is a series of choices.

- I had chosen to give birth to Sarah.
- I had chosen to make the relationship work with Andrew.
- I had chosen to move to New Zealand.
- I had chosen to do what I could to stop calves being aborted on the family farm.

These were conscious choices and as such they were the best I could make out of the options I believed were available to me at the time. But amongst these there were also a number of experiences that I had not consciously chosen.

- Sarah arriving so prematurely.
- Liam's head being engaged so long before the birth.
- The staphylococcal infection.
- Becoming involved with dairy farming.

How did these things come to be? Surely I hadn't chosen these? Or had I? Was it possible that on some level I had also chosen these experiences? I decided that it was possible but they would have had to be unconscious choices that I wasn't aware of having made. On a worldwide scale humanity is awakening, awakening from its dream; its unconsciousness. Some of us can look at different parts of the world through conscious eyes and see what the rest cannot see; the causes of the problems they are experiencing. They cannot see it though because they are 'in it' and unconscious to it. In the same way, when doing readings I can often see how someone's unconscious thoughts or beliefs cause them to have a particular experience, but clients themselves do not see it. Is it possible that a more conscious soul than I would be able to look at my life and say this is why that happened? I believe so.

I believe we are constantly making choices either consciously or unconsciously. Making them consciously with a clear intent brings them to us faster. It can help us to feel in charge of our lives or at least at cause rather than at effect. Unconscious choices make us feel that life is happening to us, that everything is out of our control and that we are powerless. Everything that happens to us is the result of a choice. If we want a different experience of reality we need to become conscious; conscious of the choices we are making moment to moment. To become conscious we simply have to be here and now and notice what is. Often, we are too busy thinking about the past or imagining our future to be here and now. If we aren't here and now, by definition, we are not making conscious choices.

Our past does not create our future, our consciousness does and the quality of our consciousness is determined by how present we are, how much of our consciousness is here and now. It is all about choice. And it is all about presence. Our power to create a new future for humanity and ourselves is here and now.

There are good choices and there are bad choices. The thing is, we only know what is good or bad for us, because only we have had our life experiences. Only we can feel how those choices feel inside. Good choices for me in terms of dairy farming would be different to good choices for someone else who is dairy farming. And that is how it is until it isn't. I cannot judge anyone else for their choices. I can only judge my own and all of us really do make the best choices we see as available to us at the time.

Choices, choices, choices. Now I understood the concept, the question was what would I choose when faced with my most important decision yet?

Accepting Responsibility

It had been nine years since a blind man called Liam had stopped me in my tracks and asked me if I accepted responsibility for what I was here to do. At the time I knew I wanted to help but I didn't know what was involved or what it would entail. Now after many years of searching for deeper understanding, investigating and learning, moving to a new country and committing myself to family life, I was ready for the next stage. I was on the verge of understanding. I was awoken in the early morning with an urge to write. I was shown that if you look at the word responsibility it is made of two words; response and ability. I was shown that I had abilities and that these abilities could be used to respond in a situation. Being responsible meant being response-able; able to respond.

I reflected on managers I had known while working for Lloyds Bank. Many had been given responsibilities such as high lending or selling targets but they were not response-able because they didn't have the skills to respond. When I had suddenly tapped into healing and psychic abilities all those years ago I started to become response-able. I had put my abilities to good use and started to explore what was possible in a really practical way. How I now chose to use those abilities was my choice.

I realised that I was different to a great many of the psychics I had met along the way. Many psychics have their abilities from birth, whereas I had the opportunity of developing my left-brain, logical, rational thinking before I started to become spiritually awakened. It meant that when I had my experiences I also questioned them and questioned myself. I had always been my own biggest cynic, constantly asking myself why these things should be happening to me as I didn't feel like I was anybody special.

As time passed I came to understand that the only reason I had developed psychic abilities was because I was open to them. The more open I allowed myself to be, the more insights I would receive and the more synchronicity I would observe in my life. I believe anyone can do this.

All the pieces of my life and the many choices I had made were suddenly fitting together. I had used the NLP (Neuro Linguistic Programming) training to heighten my self-awareness. I realised that I could not transcend what I did not know. I had to really know myself, my reactions and my unconscious programming to go beyond myself. I had consciously accelerated my own learning in terms of developing the skills for talking to the spirits of dead people and tapping into higher consciousness. Then, using my training skills developed while working for the bank, I had shared what I knew and taught others to do what I did. I had used the knowledge from the banking and marketing studies to good effect in setting up two businesses. Nothing, it appeared, was wasted. Even my time sorting cheques into alphabetical order had taught me patience.

Now it was time to choose again. I had cleared the good and bad 'karma' that I needed to clear in this lifetime. 'Karma' is an Indian word that basically means what I came into this lifetime to experience. In Buddhism it is considered that souls are pulled back into a physical lifetime again and again until they work though the unfinished karma they have to clear.

Now it was time for 'dharma'. 'Dharma' is another Indian word, this time meaning 'right action'. Knowing all that I now do, being as conscious as I am, what do I choose to do here? I spent some time reflecting on my dharmic responsibilities. I had dharmic responsibilities to my children. I had to examine what precisely I considered that meant. I had dharmic responsibilities as a partner to Andrew. Again I had to define what that meant in practice. I jotted down my thoughts. I had dharmic responsibilities as a daughter and as a sister, as a daughter-in-law and as a sister-in-law. I wrote them all down as best I could. I had dharmic responsibilities as a member of the local community, dharmic responsibilities as a citizen of New Zealand and as a human being on the earth.

My responsibility (response-ability) in each of these areas was now more than it had ever been before, as now I was a conscious mother, partner, daughter, neighbour, citizen and human being. Given all that I had experienced, what did I choose? I chose to accept the responsibility for being the best mother, partner, daughter, neighbour, citizen, human being that I could be, drawing on all that I had learnt this lifetime to assist me. Within a few days of this increased awakening I was inspired to give a public demonstration of my healing abilities to demonstrate that there is nothing that cannot be healed. I had begun on the next stage of my journey.

Perhaps, before I tell that story though, I should say that there are people who cannot be healed. This is not that these people do not deserve to be healed. Maybe one of the reasons is because they have not yet learned what they need to learn from their illness or disease. An illness showing up in your physical body is a sure sign that something isn't right on the inside. The illness might give you time out to reflect on what that wrong is. Or you can just be ill, take the pills or have the operation and not tackle the underlying issue.

I had seen this many times. One lady patient suffered with MS. She was a lovely lady, but her husband was always rather hard on her. Once she contracted MS, she was in a wheelchair and her son came over to visit her more and would take her out to places though the lady's husband was still hard on her. "It's all in your head," he would tell her.

I gave her healing on a regular basis knowing that there was no way she would get better. If she got better she would see less of her son and her husband would be able to say, "I told you it was all in your head!" She would never hear the end of it. Her trips to see me were an opportunity to be with her son as he brought her to the sessions. Was it all in this lady's head as her husband had said? No, not in the way her husband meant. But yes in another way. At some level, definitely, unconsciously, she was choosing the experience for herself.

Over the past nine years I had worked on and with people with everything from ME to terminal illnesses. Some got better and some didn't. A lady with liver cancer lived and a gentleman with lung cancer died. Why? You would have expected the odds of surviving lung cancer to be better than the chances of surviving liver cancer. I had learned a lot about how things worked, the bigger picture if you like, but I still didn't have all the answers. There were a significant number of people that didn't get well no matter what I did, though most did get well.

The public demonstration was intended to share with the wider community what I knew with the thought that maybe the people who attended could then take the learning that stage further. I knew I was to contact the Whirling Rainbow, another spiritual group in New Plymouth where I lived. I had not had contact with them before. A friend said there was no way I would be able to arrange to speak at short notice as they booked their guest speakers about six weeks in advance. Internally I knew I would be speaking there on Thursday and then doing a follow up talk to more people on the following Sunday.

My friend gave me the phone number for the organiser of the Whirling Rainbow. Sure enough when I spoke to the organiser, she had just put the phone down from a cancellation and was happy to book me as the replacement. I took this as the sign that I was doing what I should be doing. I knew that the public talk and demonstration would come from the heart. People had a right to know what I knew and I had a duty to share it. My personal knowledge was incomplete but I was sure it may still help some people. Higher guidance would help me find the right words when the time came.

The talk and demonstration went very well. I explained that the healing was not from me but through me and that they too could do this if they wished. The energies were good and a number of people received significant healings. The funniest was an older gentleman who had trouble with one of his knees. At the start it was painful and stiff to bend while ten to fifteen minutes later it was perfectly fine. He lay on the couch waving his leg in the air. He hadn't been able to do that for years. His wife, who was in the audience agreed and the audience laughed. Now it seemed everyone wanted a try on the couch. It was very late by the time I was able to finally leave and though I was tired, I was happy with how the evening had gone.

An even larger audience awaited me on the following Sunday evening and that too went well. I had a long list of names and phone numbers of people wishing to see me privately for healing. The gentleman with the healed knee from the first demonstration came to see me the following week to 'fix' his other one. He hadn't realised that the second one hurt too until the first one was fixed. The healing went well and I had a happy client and an even happier wife.

Another man who heard about the first gentleman's knees came to see me. He had similar problems with his knees and hoped I would be able to help. Over the years I had learned that when energy got stuck in the knees it was usually a sign of stubbornness. As the gentleman lay on the couch, I asked him, "If I were to ask your wife how stubborn you were on a scale of zero to one hundred, with one hundred being completely pig-headed, what would she say?"

"Ninety-seven!" came the response. I was very likely wasting my time, but it wasn't for me to prejudge the situation. Everyone can change if they want to. We tried two more treatments and I talked with him about the link between the inflexibility of his knees and his inflexibility with his family. He didn't want to change. He was being stubborn about being stubborn and his knees continued to trouble him.

I was busy as a healer for several months following the demonstrations. I also ran workshops, starting to show people how to do what I did. Healing is a natural ability we can all tap into for ourselves and for others.

Around this time I was also inspired to set up a charitable trust, which I called The Dharmic Trust. The name is not linked with a particular religion. It was chosen simply as the word which best conveyed for me the purpose of the charity; conscious right action would be its literal translation.

I saw this as a significant decision as life as it is meant to be lived is a sacred outpouring of action from the deepest recesses of the soul. The four initial aims of the Trust address the changes that I have been shown needing to take place with regard to education, our environment, our society and in health and science. You can find out more at www.thedhamictrust.co.nz. One of the aims is to create fabulous schools that encourage the unfoldment of the whole child and an appreciation of nature. We have made significant progress towards opening our first school. One of the aims with regard to the environment came to me completely out of the blue as an insight early one morning. I was inspired to write this;

"Genetic Engineering values competitive advantage, money, and man's limited knowledge of genetics, over the innate Divine Knowledge that is within each and every organism. It is based on a fundamentally flawed belief that these organisms are separate to us.

Until YOU truly realise (see with REAL EYES) the interconnectedness of all things you will not fully understand the implications of what you are doing.

All life contains consciousness in different stages of evolution. Each species has free will choice to determine its own evolution. Genetic Engineering, if allowed to continue, would interfere with this free will choice.

Genetic Research, on the other hand would value all life and the sacredness of life.

It would value what could be learned from other species without affecting their natural state. It would value the interconnectedness of all things. It would value learning.

Your scientists are like children who have just discovered that if you mix red and yellow you get orange. That if you mix blue and yellow you get green. Is orange any better than red? Is green any better than blue? Of course not, they are just different. The discovery of orange, doesn't make red any less wonderful.

Unfortunately, we are not playing with colours here. You are playing with LIFE. By making genetic modifications to 'naturally' occurring species you are replacing the red with the orange, replacing the blue with the green.

Why?

How much better for man to live in harmony with all life and his environment.

Life has no meaning save the meaning you give it – what meaning are you giving life when you treat it this way?

I did not consciously know very much about Genetic Engineering but with this insight and then coming across an article about MAdGE – Mothers Against

Genetic Engineering in a women's magazine I decided to research it further. In much the same way that I hadn't been conscious of what dairy farming involved I wasn't conscious of what was happening with GE. The whole concept of inserting human genes into other species, which was the thrust of the article, made me cringe. Was this an emotional, irrational response or was there something fundamentally wrong with it?

I knew that from a spiritual perspective it had its problems, but what was the 'true' situation? I made it my job to find out and joined MAdGE the very next day. Joining MAdGE really opened my eyes. I found out that there were not only spiritual concerns about GE, but also some very real physical and practical concerns from scientists around the world which I couldn't believe that I had not heard about before. What I read on the different GE websites was far more newsworthy than what I was reading about in newspapers. I decided there and then to take a more active role within MAdGE and I helped set up a local group.

The group's aim was to raise local awareness about GE and in addition to talk one-to-one with people about GE, manning information stalls and writing to local papers. We joined many other groups marching one Saturday in October 2003 to protest nationally about the lifting of the moratorium on GE.

On the morning of the march, I was washing dishes when a voice in my head told me that no matter how many people marched that day the government would lift the moratorium. I was absolutely certain of this and then the voice said, "Now to Plan B". I had already been guided to hold mediumship shows to raise money for the Dharmic Trust in the following year. The money was to go to assist with the development of our vision of a new kind of school. Now this guidance was reinforced once again, but with more urgency and with another twist. Plan B was to hold mediumship shows as soon as possible to educate people of the dangers of GE and to raise funds for groups opposing the release of untested GE into the food chain and the environment.

My new responsibility (response-ability) was taking shape and happening faster than I had anticipated.

Only the week before, as if to prepare me for this, I had done my first New Zealand demonstration of mediumship to an audience of about fifty at the Spiritual Centre in New Plymouth. I was a bit rusty as it was several years since my last public mediumship demonstration. At this show, Andrew saw me work publicly for the first time and was impressed with my skill and accuracy. Working in front of a group is very different to working one-to-one as I had found during my psychic fair experiences. It takes a lot more energy and focus. I not only have to identify which of the spirits to connect with but also keep the spirits of other people at bay while I deal with one individual at a time. I have to pre-screen messages too, taking into account who may be in the audience. I can't mention affairs for example or adoption sometimes, and I have to take into account the individual's likely reaction to the message. Would it make them too emotional in front of a group? Would it cause embarrassment? I have to be more conscious, more fully present than ever before to do the work. And I have to relax or I can not bring the messages through.

I had also been the guest speaker at a Spiritualist church, which went well, but was I ready to jump from these demonstrations with groups of spiritually-minded people to a large public show? Andrew worried. He thought I should practise more whereas I, on the other hand, knew it was what I needed to do and I understood completely why I had to do it. I booked a room at a local hotel on a Sunday night and by Thursday we had sold two hundred tickets. I arranged for Bryan Vickery, a local radio and television personality with whom I had previously worked on the local television channel, to host the show for me. Bryan was an excellent presenter and openly sceptical of my claims of being able to speak with the dead. It was a healthy scepticism and he was open to being given proof.

At the hotel, getting dressed for the show, I was starting to feel nervous and asked for help. Was I doing the 'right' thing or had I totally lost the plot? As far as I had come over the last nine years I still needed reassurance and wasn't too proud to ask for it. I learnt way back during my NLP course that it was alright to ask for help. "Please give me a sign that I am doing the right thing and that everything will be alright." I said out loud and I meant it. I then took my change of underwear out of my bag and out fell a silver crucifix. It was a Celtic-style cross I had owned for many years but had not worn for a long time. How it came to be in my underwear bag, who knows, but I took it as a sign that the show would go well.

I was amazingly calm for my first large show. I had an enormous amount of help from the spiritual dimensions. Messages came through well and Bryan interviewed those to whom I gave messages, to see how accurate they felt I had been. Everyone gave me ten out of ten apart from one lady. She paused, reflecting on Bryan's question and then gave me twenty out of ten. The audience cheered. By the end of the first half, the audience was teasing Bryan that he was the only sceptic left in the room and that he should sit in the chair. Bryan came to see me at the interval. He said he was game, if I was. I thought it would be fun but self-doubt crept in and I wondered whether he was open enough for me to get a link so that I could do it. I link with spirit through the living person so to link with Bryan's relatives in spirit world I had to go through his energy field. If he was tense or closed I wouldn't be able to get any links. I hardly had a chance to say that I was prepared to give it a go, before Bryan, who was keen to start the second half, was on his way out into the chair.

The first half had gone so well, I asked internally for help again. "Please help me to do as well in the second half." The audience was clapping and out I went to face Bryan in the chair.

"Don't say anything about ex-girlfriends," he joked.

"We'd be here all night," quipped a female member of the audience. Humour. Of course! That was how I would do it. If he was laughing, whether he was cynical or not, he would be open. Then I could be sure to find the link with his loved ones in spirit. I asked for his watch. Psychometry always helps me if I am feeling nervous or finding it hard to make a link.

"It's from The Warehouse (a cheaper chain of stores)," he joked as he handed it over. The audience laughed. They hadn't expected a local celebrity to be wearing a watch from The Warehouse.

"You can tell a lot about a person from their watch," I said, holding it up to show the audience. Bryan's watch was purple and plastic! Bryan and the audience were rolling in their seats, tears were rolling down my eyes and I had a link. I had his grandfather on his dad's side with me. He was shaking his head about New Zealand rugby. I was also shown that he wasn't from New Zealand.

"I have your grandfather on your father's side with you," I began. Bryan sat up straighter, his face becoming more serious. "Does that make sense?" Yes, Bryan had to admit it did. "And he doesn't come from here, not from New Zealand. Why is he shaking his head about New Zealand rugby?" Bryan reluctantly admitted that his grandfather was Australian and that his father had played Australian Rules rugby professionally. He understood why his grandfather would be shaking his head about traditional English rugby.

The only other message was, "Wells". I didn't understand it but I said it because I got it. Bryan went white. Wells was the name of his ex-wife. He had told me not to mention the girlfriends. His grandfather thought it would be funny to mention his ex-wife! The audience loved it but it was not the highlight of the show. That was yet to come.

Before the show I'd had so many things to do that I am sure I was deliberately being kept busy to keep me from getting nervous. One of the stops I made was at a local florist I had not visited before. I knew that I had to go in and order a bouquet of red roses, to give to someone at the show but I couldn't understand the reason. I just trusted it and bought them.

When I returned to collect the roses the florist had painted them in gold leaf on the edges of the petals and sprinkled golden glitter on them. It must have taken the florist ages. She certainly took a pride in her work. They looked beautiful, but I had only wanted red roses. I hoped that they would be alright.

Now, in the second half of the show, I had a lady sitting on stage with me and her father in spirit world wanted to give her red roses. I suddenly realised that I may have found the reason why I had bought the red roses. I asked her, "Why would Dad be wanting to give you red roses?" and she explained that her dad's nickname for her was Rosie even though it was not her birth name. The hairs on my arms stood on end. I knew I had found the recipient for the flowers but that I should give them to her near the end of the show as it was going to be very emotional.

When the end of the show came, Andrew went to get the roses and I made my way with the microphones, to the back of the room where 'Rosie' was sitting. I shared with the audience the story of the roses. How I had had to stop the car at this particular florist and how they had been painted with gold paint when I returned. "Rosie, I know that these flowers are for you sweetheart, but what I don't know is why the gold paint? Why is that significant?" You could have heard a pin drop. Andrew passed a microphone to Rosie. It took her a few moments before she could speak. "My dad died just after his golden wedding anniversary," Rosie explained.

It was a very emotional moment, for everyone. It was so humbling to think how spirit can work through not only me but a florist and through Rosie, bringing her to the show so that she could get her message.

"I knew I had to come tonight," Rosie told me later privately. "I had felt Dad with me all day." It was the perfect ending to my first show. Bryan, my sceptical host was so impressed he even mentioned the show as a news item on the radio next day.

My first mediumship show had been a success and reaffirmed my commitment to this direction. I was pleased that my mediumship skills were still strong and I was able to receive accurate messages readily. It was rewarding to be able to bring such peace and closure to many. I cried a lot in the next few days and found myself spontaneously jumping in the air, literally jumping for joy. I was so grateful for all the help I had received along the way that had got me to this point. I reflected back on Alison Harper's words of some years ago when she'd 'seen' me on stage in front of hundreds of people working for a charity. The future she had seen for me was now reality. In subsequent shows I was even to wear the blue dress she'd predicted. I remember telling a good friend what it was I was going to do; that I was going to work as a medium in front of hundreds of people. "Whatever would posses you to do that?" she asked, pulling a face.

"I know it is not what everyone would choose, but it is absolutely what I love to do," I said.

Unexpectedly, I came across something I had written down a long time ago. It was a quotation by Eva Pierakkos.

'The incarnating soul meets with her spirit guides to plan the coming lifetime. In this meeting the soul and the guides consider the tasks she needs to accomplish in soul growth, what karma needs to be met and dealt with, and the negative belief systems she needs to clear through experience. This life work is usually referred to as a person's task. The amount of counselling a soul has from her guides in determining her future life-circumstances depends on her maturity.

Parents are chosen who will provide the needed environmental and physical experience. These choices determine the mixture of energies that will eventually form the physical vehicle in which the soul will incarnate for its task. These energies are very precise and equip the soul with exactly what it needs for its task.

The soul takes on both a personal task of personal learning and a 'world task' which entails a gift for the world. The design is so unique that by fulfilling the personal task one becomes prepared to fulfil the world task. The personal task frees the soul by releasing energies that are then used for the world task.'

I knew that I was at last consciously doing what I came here to do. My personal task and my world task were intertwined; I had to face my own fears and live my truth and in doing so I had automatically embarked on my world task.

Today I travel around the world sharing my truth; that there is no death and that we are eternal. I do this by passing on messages from loved ones about things I could not possibly know. I use my abilities for what I still consider is the highest possible reason; raising humanity's consciousness. I write most days about my journey and its lessons, to share my insights through a series of books I am working on. The proceeds from the work I do goes into the charitable trust to real-ise (make real) some of the dreams I share with many others, into physical reality. I am finally realising my life goal that I had established during the NLP course to 'dream incredible dreams and manifest them'. I have my Dream Foundation and I am beginning to put into place ideas that will benefit humanity.

If I can access this level of love and wisdom within me, you can too as we are all part of the same wonderful creation. To tap in though you have to be present here and now and not in your mind worrying about what has happened or what might happen. It is all about becoming conscious of who we truly are, here and now and releasing the fears and illusions that keep us from being less than we are.

I know that my personal task and my world task will continue to be intertwined for some years to come. In pushing back my boundaries of what I consider is possible I also extend myself into my world task and we all have one, whether we are conscious of it or not. I continue to observe incredible synchronicity in my life as it continues to unfold and I marvel at this incredible creation we call life. It truly is a marvel that you and I are part of this reality; not passive bystanders but co-creators of our experience.

I don't always understand why certain things happen and I certainly don't have all the answers, but I do know how to listen; to listen to loved ones who have passed over, to listen to my higher guidance and listen to my feelings. There isn't a person on the planet who cannot do these things. We all have voices in our heads. We all have feelings. It is all about how conscious we choose to be to what is going on within us and around us.

One of my favourite quotes is by Wang Yang Ming; 'To know and not to do is not yet to know.'

It reminds me that consciousness on its own is not sufficient. We also need to exercise our free will choice, to care or not care about ourselves and one another, to care or not to care about this special place we call Earth.

I chose to be conscious and I chose to care.

I choose to be conscious and I choose to care.

For me there is no going back.

Good luck! Good luck!

1. His knee continued to be pain free for the rest of the course and my last contact with him, a postcard many months later, advised that he was still pain free and very grateful.

2. Perhaps at this stage I should explain the difference between the two. A clairvoyant has clear seeing in that they can see your past, present and future. A medium can see and talk with your loved ones in spirit world and give evidence to prove that there is no death and that your loved ones are in fact still around you. The evidence tends to be a mix of information you know, such as their name, how they died and their relationship to you, but often some information that you do not know will also be given. This is so that you can be sure that it is not simply mind-reading.

Personally I also ask for a piece of information about the person that is really recent and that I could not possibly know. That just shows you that your loved ones are indeed still watching over you.

3. Bible references:

Mark 9: 2 - 8. Matthew 17: 1 - 8. Luke 9: 28 - 36.

Look out for Jeanette's next book, here's just a sample!

"I can't take my mum home like this." The young girl was very close to tears and steadfast in her resolve. I sat down with the young girl's Mum. She eagerly passed me over a photograph and as she did the name Brian popped into my head. Brian was enthusiastic in his response and immediately started to put all his energy and attention into my teeth. I knew he had not died from something wrong with his teeth so I was confused as to what his message could mean. I asked his wife if she had something wrong with her teeth.

After telling me her teeth were fine she explained that before her husband died they had agreed to let each other know there was an after life by singing a particular song. She wanted me to sing the song. I asked Brian to tell me the name of the song. Again my teeth started feeling funny. I was becoming a bit frustrated now. Firmly, I asked Brian to concentrate on giving me the name of song.

Nothing, an absolute blank. Was he trying to give me the 'Sound of Silence'? My teeth started tingling again and as they did a tune started to form in my mind, a childhood song I could remember my mother singing. Where was it coming from, surely it had no meaning to this couple? It wasn't a romantic song but it was the only song I had been given. I decided to sing the first few bars.

As I sang "You're a pink toothbrush, I'm a blue toothbrush, Have we met somewhere before? You're a pink toothbrush and I think toothbrush, That we met by the bathroom door . . ." The tears spilled down the lady's face and then down her daughters. Of all the possible songs, and there must be thousands of them I had sung the very one her husband had promised to sing. I had given her the exact proof she had wanted so desperately.